> "America's leading source of self-help legal information." ★★★★
> —YAHOO!

LEGAL INFORMATION ONLINE ANYTIME

24 hours a day

www.nolo.com

AT THE NOLO.COM SELF-HELP LAW CENTER, YOU'LL FIND

- Nolo's comprehensive Legal Encyclopedia filled with plain-English information on a variety of legal topics
- Nolo's Law Dictionary—legal terms <u>without</u> the legalese
- Auntie Nolo—if you've got questions, Auntie's got answers
- The Law Store—over 250 self-help legal products including: Downloadable Software, Books, Form Kits and eGuides
- Legal and product updates
- Frequently Asked Questions
- NoloBriefs, our free monthly email newsletter
- Legal Research Center, for access to state and federal statutes
- Our ever-popular lawyer jokes

Quality LAW BOOKS & SOFTWARE FOR EVERYONE

Nolo's user-friendly products are consistently first-rate. Here's why:

- A dozen in-house legal editors, working with highly skilled authors, ensure that our products are accurate, up-to-date and easy to use
- We continually update every book and software program to keep up with changes in the law
- Our commitment to a more democratic legal system informs all of our work
- We appreciate & listen to your feedback. Please fill out and return the card at the back of this book.

OUR "NO-HASSLE" GUARANTEE

Return anything you buy directly from Nolo for any reason and we'll cheerfully refund your purchase price. No ifs, ands or buts.

An Important Message to Our Readers

This product provides information and general advice about the law. But laws and procedures change frequently, and they can be interpreted differently by different people. For specific advice geared to your specific situation, consult an expert. No book, software or other published material is a substitute for personalized advice from a knowledgeable lawyer licensed to practice law in your state.

Nondisclosure Agreements:

Protect Your Trade Secrets and More

by Attorneys Richard Stim
and Stephen Fishman

Keeping Up-To-Date

To keep its books up-to-date, Nolo issues new printings and new editions periodically. New printings reflect minor legal changes and technical corrections. New editions contain major legal changes, major text additions or major reorganizations. To find out if a later printing or edition of any Nolo book is available, call Nolo at 510-549-1976 or check our website at http://www.nolo.com.

To stay current, follow the "Update" service at our website at http://www.nolo.com/update. In another effort to help you use Nolo's latest materials, we offer a 35% discount off the purchase of the new edition of your Nolo book when you turn in the cover of an earlier edition. (See the "Special Upgrade Offer" in the back of the book.)

First Edition	OCTOBER 2001
Editor	MARY RANDOLPH
Book Design and Production	SUSAN PUTNEY
Cover Designer	TONI IHARA
Index	THÉRÈSE SHERE
Proofreading	SHERYL ROSE
Printing	CONSOLIDATED PRINTERS, INC.
Illustrations	SASHA STIM-VOGEL

Fishman, Stephen.
    Nondisclosure agreements : protect your trade secrets & more / by Richard Stim & Stephen Fishman.
       p. cm.
   Includes index.
   ISBN 0-87337-646-3
    1. Trade secrets—United States. 2. Covenants (Law)--United States. I. Fishman, Stephen.
II. Title.
KF3197.Z9 F57 2001
346.7304'8--dc21   2001016412

For information on bulk purchases or corporate premium sales, please contact the Special Sales Department. For academic sales or textbook adoptions, ask for Academic Sales. Call 800-955-4775 or write to Nolo, 950 Parker Street, Berkeley, CA 94710.

Acknowledgments

The authors wish to thank:

Mary Randolph for her concise editing

Toni Ihara for her attractive cover design

Susan Putney for making the book look sharp

Sasha Vogel-Stim for her fresh illustrations

About the Authors

Attorney **Richard Stim** has represented artists, photographers, musicians and software and multimedia businesses. He is the author of several Nolo books, including *License Your Invention, Music Law,* and *Getting Permission: How to License & Clear Copyrighted Materials Online & Off.*

After stints in government and private practice, attorney **Stephen Fishman** became a full-time legal writer in 1982. He is the author of *The Copyright Handbook, Web & Software Development, The Public Domain* and many more plain-English legal books, all published by Nolo.

Table of Contents

Introduction

Chapter 1: What NDAs Can—and Can't—Protect

Chapter 2: Using NDAs as Part of a Trade Secret Protection Program

Chapter 3: Nondisclosure Agreements: The Basics

Chapter 4: Nondisclosure Agreements for Specific Situations

Chapter 5: Who Owns a Trade Secret?

Chapter 6: If Someone Violates an NDA

Chapter 7: Noncompetition Agreements

Chapter 8: Other Ways to Protect Ideas

Appendix A

Appendix B

How to Use the CD-ROM

Appendix C

Forms and Agreements on CD-ROM

Introduction

In today's business world it's hard to avoid nondisclosure agreements (also known as NDAs). Once reserved for employees and contractors, these agreements have become so ubiquitous that couples on blind dates in Silicon Valley sometimes sign them just in case any business secrets are disclosed during the evening.

If you are like many small businesses, you think of yourself as a friend of employees and contractors. Asking people to sign a restrictive agreement such as an NDA may seem burdensome or out of character for your company. But the FBI and American Society of Industrial Security estimate that U.S. businesses lose at least $24 billion a year because of stolen trade secrets, most of it from the sale of secrets by employees to competitors. Using a nondisclosure agreement may prove to be the best method of protecting your business and its confidential information.

Unfortunately, businesses that indiscriminately use NDAs are often unaware of their limitations. The improper use of an NDA can backfire, with serious repercussions for your business. For example, if a court invalidates your NDA, a contractor or ex-employee may freely disclose secret information—a result that would certainly please your competitors.

In short, signing a document titled "Nondisclosure Agreement" will not automatically erect a shield around your business information. To protect you, an NDA must be properly drafted and must correctly identify secret information. In addition, you must take other reasonable efforts to keep your information secret.

The goal of this book is to prepare you for the realities of protecting business information and to give you a well-rounded picture of how NDAs fit into your business strategy. Although we don't provide an NDA for blind dates, we do provide many other NDAs on the CD-ROM at the back of this book. These agreements can be used in a wide range of situations in which you need to preserve your business secrets and maintain your business advantage.

NDAs are an important tool to protect against disclosure of secret information. If your information is disclosed in violation of a signed agreement, you can sue for breach of contract and obtain money to compensate you for any damages as well as a court order prohibiting further disclosure. In addition, a nondisclosure agreement confers other benefits:

- It places the party receiving the information on notice that you consider the information confidential.
- It specifies what information is defined as confidential, which helps prevent misunderstandings and resolve disputes.
- It can establish a method for resolving disputes—for example, mandating that the parties arbitrate any disputes instead of going to court.
- It can guarantee that any dispute will be decided in your geographic area.
- It can establish which state's laws will govern disputes. For example, if you are entering into an agreement with a company in another state, you may prefer to have disputes resolved under your state's trade secret laws rather than the laws of the other party's state.
- In some cases, you may have a longer period of time to file a lawsuit (see Chapter 6, Section D3) than if you did not have a signed agreement.

Keep in mind that a properly drafted nondisclosure agreement is not a panacea. It can be difficult for you to know whether an ex-employee has disclosed trade secrets to a competitor. Moreover, even if you are sure trade secrets have been disclosed, it can be difficult to obtain court relief for violations of a nondisclosure agreement.

First, you must prove that the employee actually disclosed trade secrets. (Only information that legally qualifies as a trade secret can be protected by an NDA.) This can be an onerous task, especially if the ex-employee claims that the information allegedly disclosed isn't legally a trade secret.

That's why we have not limited this book to just preparing NDAs. We also cover how to approach trade secret disputes with ex-employees, acquiring and protecting trade secrets and alternatives to NDAs, such as noncompete agreements. We help you:

- identify the information you can protect under an NDA (Chapter 1);
- ascertain which of your employees, contractors or partners should sign an NDA (Chapters 3 and 4);
- draft or modify a valid NDA suitable for your purposes without an attorney (Chapters 3 and 4);
- take other necessary steps to protect your confidential business information (Chapter 2);
- make sure you own all secret information created by your employees and contractors (Chapter 5);
- respond to the illegal disclosure of your secrets by someone who signed your NDA (Chapter 6);
- determine whether an NDA or a noncompetition agreement is better in your situation (Chapter 7); and
- protect information that otherwise might not be protected under an NDA (Chapter 8).

Icons Used in This Book

Tip *A commonsense tip to help you understand or comply with legal requirements.*

Warning *A caution to slow down and consider potential problems.*

See an Expert *A suggestion to seek the advice of an attorney or tax expert.*

Fast Track *An indication that you may be able to skip some material that may not be relevant to your situation.*

Other Resources *A reference to a book, website or other resource that may help you with a particular issue.*

Form on CD-ROM *A reference to a form included on the CD-ROM at the back of the book.*

Companion CD

Included at the back of this book is a CD-ROM containing files for the tear-out forms included in Appendix C. This CD-ROM can be used with both Windows and Macintosh computers. The files are in standard file formats that can be opened, completed, printed and saved using a word processor. For instructions on using the forms, see Appendix B

What NDAs Can—and Can't—Protect

Almost every business has some valuable confidential information that it wants to keep under wraps. It could be a sales plan, a list of customers, a manufacturing process or a formula for a soft drink. This confidential information is a form of property whose value would drop to zero if competitors knew it. In legal terms, these are your business's trade secrets. Trade secrets are the only kind of information that can be protected by an NDA.

This chapter will help you determine what types of business information you can protect with an NDA. Subsequent chapters explain how to prepare and modify nondisclosure agreements to suit your business.

⚠️ *Information that is protected under an NDA may qualify for legal protection under copyright or patent law. For more information on this intellectual property overlap, read Section D.*

A. What Is a Trade Secret?

NDAs won't protect just *any* business information; the information must qualify as a trade secret. A trade secret is born in secrecy and spends its life in concealment, disclosed only to those bound to maintain confidentiality.

Trade secrets typically include such items as:

- unpublished computer code
- product design definitions and specifications
- product development agreements and other related agreements
- business plans
- financial projections
- marketing plans
- sales data
- unpublished promotional material
- cost and pricing information
- customer lists, and
- pending patent applications.

In order for business information to qualify as a trade secret, the information must:

(1) not be generally known or ascertainable through legal methods;

(2) provide a competitive advantage or have economic value; and

(3) be the subject of reasonable efforts to maintain secrecy.

Now, let's look at each of these requirements in detail.

1. Information Not Generally Known or Legally Ascertainable

If your competitors already know the material you want to protect, it isn't much of a secret. Once it's generally known or can be learned by the people within an industry, the information loses its special status and is not protected by nondisclosure agreements.

a. Generally known

There is no clear line that shows when information is "generally known" in a particular industry. In most cases, information is generally known if it has been published or publicly displayed or is commonly used within an industry. Confidential information may be known by more than one business within an industry and still qualify as a trade secret, but if it is known by many businesses it will not qualify. For example, one court ruled that bidding procedures for the sale of fencing and guard rails did not qualify as a trade secret because any experienced bidder would be aware of the information. *Whitmyer Bros., Inc., v. Doyle*, 274 A.2d 577, 58 N.J. 25, 274 (1971).

It is also possible that information that is generally known in one industry can be a trade secret in another industry if the information is used in a novel way.

> **EXAMPLE:** A chemical sealant is commonly used in the aerospace industry for waterproofing engines. A golf club maker adopts the same sealant. The sealant provides golfers with more control over the ball's drive. Within the aerospace industry the information cannot be a trade secret. But because the novel use on golf clubs is not generally known within the sporting equipment industry, it qualifies as a trade secret. To ensure that the information remains a trade secret, the golf club manufacturer should use NDAs with its research scientists and any other parties privy to the information.

Similarly, publicly known information can be a trade secret if it is compiled or assembled in a unique manner. For example, in one case, a court protected a combination of generic public domain computer programs linked together in a unique way not generally known outside the business. *Integrated Cash Management Serv., Inc. v. Digital Transactions*, 920 F.2d 171 (2d Cir. 1990).

b. Readily ascertainable

Information is "readily ascertainable" if it can be obtained legally within an industry—for example, if you can find it through an online database, at a library or through other publicly available sources. For instance, a Washington court ruled that a casino's profit margin and community contributions were not trade secrets because the information could be obtained by visiting the casino, reading newspaper articles or speaking with agencies that received mandatory community service contributions from the casino. *Confederated Tribes v. Johnson,* 135 Wash. 2d 734, 958 P.2d 260 (1998).

A trade secret is not readily ascertainable if bribery, fraud or other deceptive procedures are required to get it. Some examples of improper means include:

- Obtaining the secret from a supplier, consultant, financial advisor or other person who signed a nondisclosure agreement.
- Stealing it through industrial espionage such as electronic surveillance, bribery or tapping a company's phone lines or computers.
- Learning it from an employee who changes jobs and discloses the secret to a new employer.

For more on improper means of getting information. see Chapter 6.

State laws may prohibit employees from stealing trade secrets even in the absence of nondisclosure agreements. (See Chapter 6.)

The issue of whether a trade secret is readily ascertainable often arises when an NDA is used to prevent disclosure of a customer list. A business argues that an employee stole a customer list; the employee claims that the customer list is readily ascertainable. If it is, an NDA will not prevent the employee from disclosing the information because it does not qualify as a trade secret. For example, one court permitted an employee to use a former employer's customer list since the information was readily derived from a telephone directory. *USAchem, Inc. v. Goldstein*, 512 F.2d 163 (2d Cir. 1975). For more on customer lists, see Section B7.

2. The Information Provides Economic Value or a Competitive Advantage

To protect business information under an NDA, the information must have some economic value or provide an advantage over competitors. For most trade secrets, this requirement is easy to fulfill and can be demonstrated by benefits derived from the use of the trade secret, the costs of developing the secret, or by business or licensing offers for use of the secret.

Another way of assessing the competitive edge or value of a trade secret is to ask whether a business would be damaged if a competitor acquired the information. For example, one trade secret in the pizza industry—the process for freezing pre-cooked sausage—was the subject of a legal dispute. A court determined that the information was a valuable secret, and a jury awarded $10.9 million in lost profits to the meat packer from whom it had been stolen. *C&F Packing Co. v. IBP, Inc.,* 1994 U.S. Dist. LEXIS 973 (N.D. Ill. 1994).

A trade secret loses its economic value after public disclosure or in some cases, after the passage of time.

EXAMPLE: CommCo owns a trade secret for connecting teletype machines. The trade secret has lost its value because teletype machines have been replaced in the communications industry by computers and fax machines.

3. The Company Has Taken Reasonable Steps to Protect the Information

You cannot protect information under an NDA unless you have taken reasonable precautions to keep the information confidential. These precautions usually involve reasonable security procedures as well as the use of nondisclosure agreements. If you don't maintain reasonable security, the information will lose its trade secret status. For example, a federal court of appeals ruled that a blood bank did not keep its list of blood donors sufficiently confidential when it posted the list on a computer bulletin board accessible to its competitors. *American Red Cross v. Palm Beach Blood Bank, Inc.,* 143 F.3d 1407 (11th Cir. 1998).

In general, a business is considered to have taken reasonable steps if it uses a sensible system for protecting information—for example, locking its facilities, monitoring visitors and labeling confidential information. (We provide some suggestions for a trade secret maintenance system in Chapter 2.)

A crucial part of your company's trade secret maintenance should be to require contractors, employees, investors and others exposed to confidential information to enter into a nondisclosure agreement. If the secret is disclosed you can sue the loose-lipped person for money damages and ask for a court order preventing further disclosure.

B. Examples of Information Protected by NDAs

NDAs can protect a variety of confidential information. Here are some examples of protectible trade secrets.

1. Processes

Chemical, mechanical and manufacturing processes are commonly protected under nondisclosure agreements. Examples include processes for manufacturing chocolate powder, chicken pox vaccine or marble picture frames.

2. Business Strategies and Methods

Business strategies such as marketing schemes, advertising campaigns, business plans and new product announcements can be protected as trade secrets. For example courts have held that marketing strategies for the sale of propane gas and a business plan for a new franchise are trade secrets. A business method—a manner of conducting business or a way of doing business—is also a protectible trade secret. Examples of business methods include a system for analyzing mortgage rates or a process for instructing employees.

3. Designs, Blueprints and Specifications

Designs for products, machines and structures, or other manufacturing specifications, can be protected as trade secrets.

Examples include the design for a photo-processing machine, the blueprint for a casino or specifications for a paint roller.

4. Formulas

Formulas are an obvious choice for trade secret protection—the most well-known is the secret combination of flavoring oils and other ingredients that give Coca-Cola its distinctive taste (referred to by the company as "Merchandise 7X"). Other formulas that could be protected as trade secrets include pharmaceutical, chemical and cosmetic compounds.

5. Physical Devices and Articles

Physical devices such as machines, devices or objects can be subject to trade secret protection. Usually, trade secret protection is lost once the device is made public, but protection may enable you to protect it before obtaining a patent or while attempting to sell or license the product.

6. Computer Software

Computer software is commonly protected under trade secret law because the underlying software code is not readily ascertainable or generally known. A computer program often qualifies for trade secret status during its development and testing stage. (It may also qualify for protection under copyright or patent law.)

7. Customer Lists

Companies are often very eager to protect their customer lists with NDAs, particularly when a former employee might use a customer list to contact clients. If a dispute over a customer list ends up in court, a judge generally considers the following elements to decide whether or not a customer list qualifies as a trade secret:

- Is the information in the list ascertainable by other means? A list that is readily ascertainable cannot be protected.
- Does the list include more than names and addresses? For example, a customer list that includes pricing and special needs is more likely to be protected because this information adds value.
- Did it take a lot of effort to assemble the list? A customer list that requires more effort is more likely to be protected under an NDA.
- Did the departing employee contribute to the list? If the departing employee helped create it or had personal contact with the customers, it is less likely to be protected under an NDA.
- Is the customer list personal, long-standing or exclusive? If a business can prove that a customer list is special to its business and has been used for a long time, the list is more likely to be protected.

EXAMPLE 1: A salesman worked for an insurance company selling credit life insurance to automobile dealers. When he switched jobs to work for a competing insurance company he took his customer list and contacted the customers at his new job. A court ruled that the customer list was not a trade secret because the names of the automobile dealers were easily ascertainable by other means and because the salesman had contributed to the creation of the list. *Lincoln Towers Ins. Agency v. Farrell*, 99 Ill. App. 3d 353, 425 N.E.2d 1034 (1981).

EXAMPLE 2: Former employees took the client list of a temporary employee service. The former employees argued that the list could not be a trade secret since the information could be obtained through other means. A court disagreed and prevented the ex-employees from using the list because it could not be shown, using public information, which companies were likely to use temporary employees and because the list also included such information as the volume of the customer's business, specific customer requirements, key managerial customer contacts and billing rates. *Courtesy Temporary Serv., Inc. v. Camacho*, 222 Cal. App. 3d 1278 (1990).

Wholesalers' lists of retail concerns are often hard to protect as trade secrets. Retailers are usually easy to identify through trade directories and other sources, and a list of them ordinarily does not confer a competitive advantage. But there are exceptions—for instance, a list of bookstores that order certain types of technical books and pay their bills promptly may be very valuable to a wholesale book distributor. But if the information is readily ascertainable through trade publications or other industry sources, it is not classified as a trade secret.

In a California case, a court determined that employees who left a business could use their former employer's mailing list to send out an announcement of their change of employment to former clients. The former employer's mailing list was not a trade secret because: (1) the clients became known to the ex-employees through personal contacts; *and* (2) the use of the customer list simply saved the ex-employees the minor inconvenience of looking up the client addresses and phone numbers. In other words, the information was easy to ascertain. *Moss, Adams & Co. v. Shilling*, 179 Cal. App. 3d 124 (1984).

8. Collections of Data

A database—information of any type organized in a manner to facilitate its retrieval—is often protected as a trade secret. For example, a court ruled that a da-

tabase for inventorying and cost econo-
mies on wholesale sandwich production
for fast-food retailers was a protectible
trade secret. *One Stop Deli, Inc. v.
Franco's, Inc.*, 1994-1 CCH Trade Cas. P
70,507 (W.D. Va. 1993). A collection of
data that is readily ascertainable, however,
is not a trade secret.

Databases may also be protected under
copyright law if the method of compiling
or arranging the data is sufficiently creative.

 Web and Software Development: A
Legal Guide *by Attorney Stephen
Fishman (Nolo) explains how databases
can be protected.*

9. Know-How

Know-how does not always refer to secret
information. Sometimes it means a particular kind of technical knowledge that may
not be confidential but that is needed to
accomplish a task. For example, an
employee's know-how may be necessary
to train other employees in how to make
or use an invention. Although know-how
is a combination of secret and nonsecret
information, we suggest that you treat it as
a protectible trade secret. If you disclose
know-how to employees or contractors,
use a nondisclosure agreement.

10. Miscellaneous Business Information

Costs, pricing, new product names, information regarding new business opportuni-
ties, personnel performance, sales information, books and records of business are
among the myriad types of business information that are also considered trade secrets.

C. When Trade Secrets Cannot Be Protected By an NDA

There are some situations when even a
signed NDA will not allow you to stop the
disclosure or use of your secret business
information. Your information will not be
protected as a trade secret if:

- you did not use reasonable efforts to
  maintain secrecy
- the trade secret information is generally known or readily ascertainable
- the trade secret is learned through
  independent discovery; or
- the trade secret is lawfully acquired
  through reverse engineering.

We have already discussed the first two
standards in Sections A3 and A1. Here we
discuss independent discovery and reverse
engineering. In both cases, trade secret
protection is lost because the information
has been discovered through legal means.

1. Independent Discovery

Anyone who creates the same secret information independently—even if it is identical to your business' trade secret—is free to use and disclose that information. In other words, creating a trade secret, by itself, does not grant you exclusive rights to use that secret.

> **EXAMPLE:** Dudely Company and Manly Company sell competing after-shave products. Dudely creates a database that compares different brands of after-shave advertising and resulting annual sales. Dudely uses this trade secret information to determine how to allocate its advertising budget. Manly's president independently creates a similar database and publishes it in a business book. Dudely will be unable to protect its formula under existing NDAs because its database is no longer a trade secret.

To preserve a possible claim of independent discovery, many companies will not look at materials furnished by an outsider who wants to sell something to the company. By refusing to consider unsolicited materials, the company has a better argument for its independent creation of similar products. One method of proving independent creation is to use clean room techniques (see "Clean Rooms" below)

 If you want the exclusive right to use and sell a secret process or invention, patent law may be a more effective means of protection. See Section D, below.

Clean Rooms

To create evidence that a company independently developed trade secrets, the company may employ clean room techniques, most of which involve isolating engineers or designers and filtering information to them. The engineers or designers are usually given an objective (for example, to create a software program that sends information from a wireless device to a computer) and are then presented with publicly available materials, tools and documents. The progress of the development team is carefully monitored and documented, and a technical expert or legal monitor reviews any requests for further information by the team. Records of the clean room development are saved to demonstrate that trade secrets were independently developed and to refute any claims that the work was copied.

2. Reverse Engineering

It is not a violation of trade secret law to disassemble and examine products that are available to the public. Trade secrets that are learned in this manner can be freely used, and the trade secret protection is lost once the information becomes publicly known.

> **EXAMPLE:** Dudely and Manly sell competing after-shave products. Manly creates a new *Macho* cologne with an odor of cigarettes and gasoline. The formula for *Macho* cologne is a trade secret. Dudely purchases a bottle of *Macho;* one of its chemists examines the product, learns its formula and publishes it on the Internet. Manly will be unable to protect its formula under existing NDAs because the formula is no longer a trade secret.

Trade secret protection is not lost simply because a trade secret *could* be discovered by reverse engineering. For example, it's not enough to claim that anyone could easily reverse engineer the trade secret material.

> **EXAMPLE:** The Food and Drug Administration (FDA) made a determination that a secret ingredient in a product was not a trade secret because it could easily be discovered by reverse engineering. A federal court later overruled the FDA determination because despite the fact that the secret could

have been discovered, no competitor *had* ever discovered the ingredient. *Zotos Int'l, Inc. v. Young,* 830 F.2d 350 (D.C. Cir. 1987).

To some extent, an NDA can be used to prevent reverse engineering, at least among those parties who sign an NDA. For example, if you enter into a nondisclosure agreement with a contractor, the contractor cannot reverse engineer the trade secret in order to circumvent the agreement. However, anyone who has not signed an NDA can freely reverse engineer the information.

D. Using NDAs to Protect Inventions, Creative Works and Trademarks

Trade secrets are part of a family of law known as intellectual property, which also includes patents, copyrights and trademarks. The types of intellectual property protection are not discrete and often overlap. For example, a process of transporting eggs on a conveyor belt can be a trade secret until it is disclosed during the patent application process. Once a patent is issued, the process is public but protected by the patent. A television game show about survivors on a desert island may be copyrighted but the name of the winner may be a trade secret until announced on the air. Below we discuss how NDAs are used when trade secrets, patents, copyrights and trademarks overlap.

1. Utility Patents

There are three types of patents—utility patents, design patents and plant patents—but we will discuss only the most common, utility patents, which protect any novel and useful invention. The term "invention" is quite broad and includes anything under the sun made by humans except for abstract ideas. Utility patents can be granted for a process (such as sterilizing surgical equipment or a method for collecting sales data on the Internet); a machine (such as a gearshift in a rowing machine); an article of manufacture (such as a pencil or a garden rake); composition of matter (such as Teflon or WD-40); or an improvement on an existing invention.

A patent allows the inventor the exclusive right to stop others from making, using and selling the invention. Patent attorney David Pressman, in his book *Patent It Yourself* (Nolo), calls the utility patent a "hunting license." It gives the inventor the right to hunt infringers and sue for damages and other legal remedies.

A utility patent is obtained by filing a patent application with the U.S. Patent and Trademark Office (PTO), meeting the standards of that agency's examiners and paying the appropriate filing, issuance and maintenance fees. The Patent and Trademark Office will not consider an invention novel if the application for the patent is made more than one year after sale, public disclosure, use or offer of sale in the United States, or if it is patented anywhere in the world. In other words, you have one year from the first sale or public disclosure to file your patent application!

Qualifying for a Utility Patent

To qualify for a utility patent, an invention must be

- useful—that is, be capable of performing its intended purpose;

- novel—that is, it must differ in some way from the publicly known or existing knowledge in the field of the invention; and

- nonobvious—that is, persons working in the field of the invention would consider the invention unexpected and surprising.

2. Should You Apply for a Patent or Keep Your Secret Information Secret?

Everything that qualifies for a patent also can qualify as a trade secret. However, you can't have both patent and trade secret protection simultaneously because the patent process requires, at some point, public disclosure of the invention. If you have a patentable invention, you must decide whether to seek the powerful protection of a patent or to maintain the invention as a trade secret. Here are some considerations:

- Patent protection lasts for approximately 17 years; trade secret protection lasts for as long as the material remains secret.
- Trade secret rights can be acquired immediately, but it often takes several years to acquire a patent.
- Trade secrets can cover more information than a patent, which is limited to one general statement of the invention and its details.
- Patent protection allows you to stop anyone from making, using, or selling the invention; a trade secret owner can stop only those who acquire the secret improperly.
- Patent protection generally entails about $5,000 to $10,000 of attorney fees to obtain; trade secret protection is relatively inexpensive.
- If you don't patent an invention, and someone else legitimately does, that person may sue you later for patent infringement. Patent laws provide some defenses but it is very possible that you could be liable for patent infringement.

 Patent It Yourself *by patent attorney David Pressman (Nolo) explains how to prepare a patent application without the aid of an attorney.*

Many companies use NDAS to protect their patentable inventions or processes as trade secrets in the initial stages of development and then seek patent protection. A patent application is published verbatim when the patent issues or earlier, as discussed below, and at that point all of the trade secrets and know-how become public. This public disclosure doesn't usually hurt the inventor, because the patent can be used to prevent anyone else from commercially exploiting the underlying information.

Every pending patent application filed on or after November 29, 2000 is published for the public to view 18 months after its filing date (or earlier if requested by the applicant). The only exception is if the applicant, at the time of filing, informs the PTO that the application will not be filed abroad. If the patent application is published and later rejected you will be in the unfortunate position of having lost both trade secret and patent rights.

If you file a patent application and want to keep it as a trade secret even if the patent isn't granted, you will have to withdraw the application before publication to prevent loss of trade secret status.

You may not need to disclose all your trade secret information when you apply for a patent. For example, you could keep confidential the research method by which you arrived at your conclusions or test results.

3. Trade Secrets and Copyrights

Copyright protects writing, music, artwork, computer programs, photographs and other forms of artistic expression. Under copyright law, the creator of an original work (known as the author) owns the exclusive right to make copies and to prevent others from copying the work or creating a derivative work (a work that is derived from or based on the author's protected work).

Copyright and trade secret laws sometimes protect the same kinds of information and sometimes are mutually exclusive. Usually, the same protection cannot exist simultaneously because copyrightable works are commonly distributed to the public or publicly displayed, thereby ending trade secret protection. However, trade secret protection may exist for copyrightable works that are not published or displayed.

Copyrights, Trade Secrets and Software

Trade secret and copyright protection may both be available for works that are distributed on a restricted basis under a copyright licensing arrangement requiring the licensee (user) to recognize and maintain the trade secret aspects of the work. This dual protection is pertinent for computer software because the distribution of a software program does not require disclosing all of the software code. The undisclosed code is a trade secret and is protected because a user commonly signs a license agreement promising not to divulge secrets in the program. Trade secret protection is generally not available for software if the source code is made available to the public on an unrestricted basis—for example, in a computer magazine or on a CD.

	Trade Secret	Copyright
What's covered	Valuable business information that is not generally known or readily ascertainable	Any original fixed work, published or unpublished
What's prohibited	Acquisition or disclosure by improper means	Unauthorized duplication, sale, distribution, publication, display or adaptation

You automatically own the copyright for any original work, even if you don't register your copyright with the U.S. Copyright Office. But because registration offers benefits, most people want to register their copyright, which requires sending a copy of the work to the Copyright Office. Once you do that, your trade secret is out unless you in some way mask the trade secret. For instance, it is possible to deposit samples of source code with major portions blacked out so that the parts of the code being maintained as a trade secret are not disclosed. There are several other methods for simultaneously registering a computer program and maintaining trade secrets. One common way is to withhold the source code altogether and deposit object code, which is impossible to understand when read in the U.S. Copyright Office.

Database Protection

Copyright law protects unpublished and published collections of information such as databases if the material is arranged in a creative manner. For example, a typical white pages phone book will not be protected because there is no creativity in alphabetizing names. Trade secret law does not require creativity in order to protect databases. A database will qualify as a trade secret if the information is not generally known or readily ascertainable.

 For more information on copyright, read The Copyright Handbook, *by Stephen Fishman (for written works),* Copyright Your Software, *by Stephen Fishman (for software and computer-related expressions), and* Web and Software Development: A Legal Guide, *also by Stephen Fishman. Nolo publishes all three books. Also, the Copyright Office, Washington, DC 20559, provides free information and copyright forms at www.loc.gov or 202-707-9100.*

4. Trade Secrets and Trademarks

Trademark law protects the right to exclusively use a name, logo or any device that identifies and distinguishes products or services. In addition to names and logos, trademark law can be used to protect trade dress and product configuration. Trade dress is the product's packaging—all the elements that give your product or service's appearance an identifiable quality, such as the combination of color, geometric shapes, imagery and lettering on a pain reliever bottle. Product configuration refers to the shape or design of your invention—for example, a distinctive oval-shaped stapler.

Trademark rights are not created until the public has been exposed to a product or service and its trademark, usually by its first use in commerce. That means an NDA cannot protect a trademark that is used in commerce or that is the subject of a federal trademark application published by the United States Patent and Trademark Office. An NDA can, however, protect a potential trademark—that is, a name or logo that a company plans to use—that has not been publicly disclosed.

For background on how a trademark can be registered, access the PTO at www.uspto.gov or see Trademark: Legal Care for Your Business and Product Name *by Stephen Elias (Nolo).*

Types of Intellectual Property			
	What Is Protected?	**Examples**	**Length of Protection**
Trade Secret	Formula, method, device, machine, compilation of facts or any information that is confidential and gives a business an advantage.	*Coca-Cola* formula; special method for assembling a patented invention; new invention for which patent application has not been filed.	As long as information remains confidential and functions as a trade secret.
Utility Patent	Machines, compositions, plants, processes, articles of manufacture.	Cellular telephone, the drug known as Vicodan, a hybrid daffodil, the Amazon 1-click process, a rake.	17 years from date of issue for patents filed before or on June 17, 1995; 20 years from the date of filing for patent applications filed after June 17,1995.
Copyright	Books, photos, music, recordings, fine art, graphics, videos, film, architecture, computer programs.	*The Firm* (book and movie), Andy Warhol prints, Roy Orbison's *Greatest Hits* (music recording, compact disc artwork and video), architectural plans for design of apartment building, Macromedia *Dreamweaver* program.	Life of the author plus 70 years for works created by a single author. Other works such as works made for hire, 120 years from date of creation or 95 years from first publication.
Trademark	Word, symbol, logo, design, slogan, trade dress or product configuration.	*Nike* name and distinctive swoosh logo, "What Do You Want To Do Today" slogan, *Mr. Clean* character, *Absolut* vodka bottle.	As long as business continuously uses trademark in connection with goods. Federal registrations must be renewed every 10 years.

2

Using NDAs as Part of a Trade Secret Protection Program

U sing nondisclosure agreements consistently is the single most important element of any trade secret protection program. But it's not the only element. NDAs should always be used in conjunction with other commonsense measures to ensure that your confidential information stays confidential.

A. Can You Keep a Secret?

Trade secret protection is based on the simple notion that keeping information close to the chest can provide a competitive advantage in the marketplace. But simply saying that information or know-how is a trade secret will not make it so. You must affirmatively behave in a way that manifests your desire to keep the information secret.

Some companies go to extreme lengths to keep their trade secrets secret. For example, the formula for Coca-Cola (perhaps the world's most famous trade secret) is kept locked in an Atlanta bank vault that can be opened only by a resolution of the Coca-Cola Company's board of directors. Only two Coca-Cola employees ever know the formula at the same time. Their identities are never disclosed to the public, and they are not allowed to fly on the same airplane.

Fortunately, such extraordinary secrecy measures are seldom necessary. You don't have to turn your office into an armed camp to protect your trade secrets, but you must take reasonable precautions to prevent people who are not subject to confidentiality restrictions from learning them.

How much secrecy is "reasonable"? This depends largely on two factors:

- The physical and financial size of your company. A small start-up company need not implement the same type of trade secrecy program as a Microsoft or IBM.
- The value of your trade secrets. More care should be taken to protect extremely valuable software code or marketing plans than relatively unimportant personnel information.

Someone needs to be in charge of a company's secrecy program. You can designate someone to serve as the company's security officer, or have the employees involved with each new project devise and enforce their own security plan. Either approach can work. The keys to any trade secret protection program are to devise a secrecy plan you and your employees can live with—and then stick to it.

B. Identifying Your Trade Secrets

The first step in any trade secret protection program is to identify what information and material is a company trade secret. As discussed in Chapter 1, a trade secret can be any information or know-how that gives a company an advantage over competitors who do not know or use the information.

It makes no difference in what form a trade secret is embodied. Trade secrets may be stored on computer hard disks or CD-ROMs, written down on paper or kept only in employees' memories.

Some companies conduct periodic trade secret "audits" or inventories in which they attempt to identify all the company information that should be protected as a trade secret. If you do this, it's best not to attempt to make such audits too detailed. If you overlook an important trade secret and it doesn't show up on a supposedly exhaustive list, someone might be able to claim it really wasn't a trade secret. To avoid this, don't attempt to create a detailed inventory of every piece of paper or computer file containing trade secrets. Rather, create a simpler inventory describing your trade secrets in more general terms—for example "all documents relating to XYZ Project." Be sure to periodically update this list.

Not everything is a trade secret. Some companies make the mistake of assuming that virtually all information about the company and its products is a trade secret that must be protected from disclosure to outsiders. They then find that attempting to protect such a morass of information is very expensive and burdensome, and they may end up abandoning their protection program. Use your common sense in deciding whether disclosure of a particular item of information to a competitor would really harm the company.

C. Basic Trade Secret Protection Program

Trade secrecy measures take time, cost money and can result in aggravation. In some cases, these measures lower productivity and employee morale if workers perceive that the company is spying on them or maintaining a fortress mentality. Don't adopt an overly ambitious security program that you'll be unable or unwilling to follow. It is much better to have a modest security program that you and your employees will stick to than an extravagant one that will be ignored or resented.

Here are the minimum safeguards a small company (a start-up, particularly) should take to protect its trade secrets. Follow them and if you ever need to file a lawsuit to prevent someone from using or disclosing information in violation of an NDA, a judge would likely conclude that you took reasonable precautions to prevent the public or competitors from learning about your secrets.

As your company grows, you'll want to implement some or all of the advanced secrecy measures discussed in Section D, below.

1. Use Nondisclosure Agreements

Before you give any person access to your trade secrets, make sure that he or she has signed a nondisclosure agreement. This is the single most important element of your trade secret protection program. How to draft and use NDAs is discussed in detail in Chapter 3.

2. Maintain Physical Security

Although employees or ex-employees, not industrial spies, most often misappropriate trade secrets, courts usually require that, in addition to using NDAs, a company take at least some reasonable steps to ensure the physical security of its trade secrets. At a minimum, a company should implement a "clean desk" and "locked file cabinets and desk drawers" policy. Documents containing trade secrets should not be left hanging about on desks when not in use; rather, they should be locked in desk drawers or filing cabinets. Your office should also be securely locked at the end of the day.

3. Increase Computer Security

Your computer system likely contains many trade secrets, such as financial records. It's vital to take reasonable measures to prevent unauthorized people from gaining access to the system. Here are some of the security measures you can employ. Some of these measures may be too much of a hassle, particularly for small companies. By no means are all required. But the more you employ, the safer your trade secrets will be.

- Use secret passwords, access procedures and firewalls to prevent trade secret theft from your company's file server. Change the passwords periodically, especially when an employee who knows the current passwords quits or is fired.
- Keep trade secrets in coded or encrypted form so outsiders can't read them. Inexpensive encryption programs such as PGP (Pretty Good Privacy) are readily available.
- Consider using separate computer systems, without Internet or other network access, for your most sensitive information.
- If practical, place computers, terminals and other peripherals in a physically secure location to which access is restricted—for example, in a locked office or room to which only those people who need to use them have the key.

Take Care With Email

Make certain that both you and your employees take care not to inadvertently disclose trade secrets in email. Always keep in mind that an email recipient can easily forward copies of a message to any number of others. Given the enormous volume of email and the fact that it is transmitted over the Internet in small packets rather than all at once, it's unlikely that anyone will intercept a specific email message in transit. Email is most likely to be read by unauthorized people when it is stored on a computer after it's composed and sent. It's wise to encrypt any email that contains any particularly sensitive information. This will make it difficult or impossible for your email to be read without your permission.

4. Label Information Confidential

Documents (both hard copy and electronic), software and other materials containing trade secrets should always be marked "confidential." This is the best way to alert employees and others that a document contains trade secrets. Moreover, nondisclosure agreements—including those in this book—require that trade secret documents be marked this way.

Here is some language you can use on any type of trade secret material:

> THIS [choose one: program, document, database] IS CONFIDENTIAL AND PROPRIETARY TO [your company name] AND MAY NOT BE REPRODUCED, PUBLISHED OR DISCLOSED TO OTHERS WITHOUT COMPANY AUTHORIZATION.

You should also obtain a rubber stamp reading CONFIDENTIAL and use it to mark documents when it's inconvenient to use the longer notice above.

Don't mark everything confidential. *Don't go overboard and mark everything in sight confidential. If virtually everything, including public information, is marked "confidential," a court may conclude that nothing was really confidential. It is better not to mark anything than to mark everything.*

a. Computer code

It's wise to combine a confidentiality notice with a copyright notice, like this:

> THIS PROGRAM IS CONFIDENTIAL AND PROPRIETARY TO _[your company name] AND MAY NOT BE REPRODUCED, PUBLISHED OR DISCLOSED TO OTHERS WITHOUT COMPANY AUTHORIZATION.
>
> COPYRIGHT ©[year] BY [your company name]

Or, if the work is unpublished, use a notice like this:

> THIS PROGRAM IS CONFIDENTIAL AND PROPRIETARY TO [your company name] AND MAY NOT BE REPRODUCED, PUBLISHED OR DISCLOSED TO OTHERS WITHOUT COMPANY AUTHORIZATION.
>
> COPYRIGHT © [your company name].
> THIS WORK IS UNPUBLISHED.

Mark all copies of source code with such a notice. Also, when you create source code, flowcharts or data compilations on your computer, include a notice at the beginning and end of the work and a few places in between.

b. Faxes and email

Try to keep faxing and emailing of trade secrets to a minimum. When it's unavoidable, be sure to include a confidentiality notice such as this one:

> THE MESSAGES AND DOCUMENTS TRANSMITTED WITH THIS NOTICE CONTAIN CONFIDENTIAL INFORMATION BELONGING TO THE SENDER.
>
> IF YOU ARE NOT THE INTENDED RECIPIENT OF THIS INFORMATION, YOU ARE HEREBY NOTIFIED THAT ANY DISCLOSURE, COPYING, DISTRIBUTION OR USE OF THE INFORMATION IS STRICTLY PROHIBITED. IF YOU HAVE RECEIVED THIS TRANSMISSION IN ERROR, PLEASE NOTIFY THE SENDER IMMEDIATELY.

This notice will make it clear to people receiving the fax or email that it contains trade secrets and should be treated with care. It can be placed on a fax cover sheet or at the beginning of an email message.

5. Don't Write Down Trade Secrets

Perhaps the best way to maintain a trade secret is not to write it down at all. Particularly in small companies, a good deal of sensitive information—marketing plans, for example—can be transmitted orally to those who need to know.

D. Advanced Trade Secret Protection

As your company grows and you develop increasingly valuable trade secrets, you'll want to consider taking some additional security precautions.

1. Limit Employee Access to Trade Secrets

Obviously, the fewer people who know a trade secret, the less likely it will leak out. In very small companies, particularly start-ups, it may not be possible or desirable to limit access to trade secrets, since everyone is involved in every facet of the company's operation. However, as a company grows, it's a good idea to restrict access to trade secrets to only those employees who really need to know them.

One way to control employees' access to trade secrets is to use project logs. Start by making a list of which employees need to have access to confidential materials for each of your company's ongoing projects. Create a log for each project and have every employee sign in and out each time they use confidential materials. The log should contain room for the date, the employee's name, the time in, the time out and perhaps additional information, depending on the project. The log can be maintained manually or via computer.

Using such logs won't necessarily prevent your trade secrets from being stolen by someone bent on committing trade se-

cret theft, but they will help you keep track of who has what trade secret materials and when they have them.

> **EXAMPLE:** An ex-employee stole a stack of paper upon which software code was printed. The company did not file a lawsuit until more than two years after the theft because it had not discovered the loss of the papers. The lawsuit was dismissed because the court ruled that the company should have detected the theft by using document control logs—a common practice among high technology companies dependent upon trade secrets. *Computer Assocs. Int'l v. Altai, Inc.,* 918 S.W.2d 453 (1996).

Trade Secret Project Log

Date _____

Document Title/Subject _____
_____

Employee's Name _____

Time Out _____

Time In _____

---

2. Beef Up Physical Security

In larger companies, you can take additional physical security precautions. Company trade secrets can be kept in a specified protected location or even in geographically separate facilities. Access to these areas can then be restricted. Large companies also employ security guards, surveillance cameras and perimeter fencing.

3. Restrict Photocopying

If trade secrets are written down, one of the principal means by which they can be lost is through unauthorized photocopying. Try to restrict access to photocopiers, particularly at night. One excellent method is to require key cards and passwords to use company photocopiers. Such systems allow you to keep a record of who uses the photocopier, how much and when.

In the absence of such a system, keep a logbook next to the copier and require anyone who copies a document marked "confidential" to record the following information: the date, name of person making the copy, name of the person for whom the copy is made, number of copies, and the subject matter and name of the document. In addition, a record should be kept of anyone who receives confidential copies—for example, the names could be written on a cover transmittal sheet. As always, those people should sign nondisclosure agreements.

```
┌─────────────────────────────────┐
│          Photocopy Log          │
│                                 │
│  Date _____          │
│                                 │
│  Person making copy _____  │
│                                 │
│  Person for whom copy made      │
│  _____  │
│                                 │
│  Number of Copies _____  │
│                                 │
│  Title/Subject of Document      │
│                                 │
│  _____  │
└─────────────────────────────────┘
```

A photocopy log such as this is not nearly as effective as key cards and passwords, but it's still better than nothing. It won't prevent someone from making unauthorized copies, but will at least show you who has been making authorized copies of confidential material. It also helps make it clear to your employees that photocopying trade secret materials is a big deal and should be done with care.

4. Shred Documents

Don't leave documents containing valuable trade secrets lying around in your wastepaper bins. Companies have been known to hire investigators to engage in dumpster diving at their competitors' premises. Obtain a shredding machine to effectively dispose of any documents containing trade secrets.

5. Use Noncompetition Agreements With Employees and Consultants

In addition to using NDAs, many companies also require employees and consultants to sign noncompetition agreements. These are agreements in which an employee or independent contractor agrees not to compete with you for a certain time period. See Chapter 7 for a detailed discussion of these agreements.

6. Screen Employee Publications and Presentations

A trade secret is lost if it is disclosed to the public on an unrestricted basis. Employers may inadvertently disclose trade secrets in speeches and presentations at trade shows and professional conferences. Trade secrets can even be lost through advertising—for example, a company that lists its clients in an advertising brochure cannot claim later that its customer list is a trade secret.

Companies with advanced trade secret programs screen all papers, articles and advance texts of speeches and presentations. The screening can be done by a formal committee consisting of members who, taken together, are familiar with all the company's products and trade secrets, or by individuals who specialize in a particular area.

Special care must be taken to avoid disclosing patentable inventions in articles or other publications. Patent protection in some foreign countries can be lost through such inadvertent disclosures. A disclosure in any country starts the one-year period during which a patent application must be filed in the U.S. or the right to do so is lost forever. (See Chapter 1, Section D.)

7. Control Visitors

Visitors to your company should not be allowed to wander unsupervised in areas where confidential materials are kept. Visitors who might be exposed to trade secrets should be asked to sign a nondisclosure agreement before leaving the reception area. (See Chapter 4, Section C, for a sample agreement.)

Many companies require visitors to sign a logbook—but that's a mistake. Visitors who sign in may be able to see who else has been visiting your company, which is often very sensitive information in itself.

8. Take Precautions When Hiring New Employees

Many companies have been sued for trade secrecy violations when they hired competitors' employees. For example, Borland filed such a suit against Microsoft in early 1997 when it hired several Borland employees.

This is particularly likely to occur if you hire a large number of employees from a single competitor to obtain a competitive advantage—a practice known as "raiding."

Of course it is improper to hire anyone for the purpose of gaining access to another's trade secrets. It can easily get you sued.

To prevent or defeat trade secrecy claims, it's important to hire employees in a way that shows that you did not hire any particular person for the purpose of obtaining access to trade secrets. In other words, you want to be able to show that all your employees were hired because of their qualifications and expertise, not because they knew competitors' trade secrets.

Here are some simple steps to take when hiring employees:

- Spread your hiring around—avoid targeting a specific company.
- Place advertisements for new employees that list the required qualifications and expertise; consider using a professional recruiter for particularly sensitive positions.
- Make all job applicants complete an employment application and present a resume.
- Interview all qualified job applicants, even if you already know them.
- Maintain thorough records of your hiring program.
- If you hire someone who has been exposed to a competitor's especially sensitive information, consider placing the new hire in a position where that information will not be used for a period of time.

- Require all employees to sign employment agreements containing a promise that they will not use or disclose their prior employer's confidential information. The employment agreements in this book contain such a clause.
- Make sure new employees don't bring any confidential materials from their old job.
- Obtain copies of any relevant agreements the applicant has signed with previous employers—including nondisclosure agreements, warning letters, invention assignment agreements and termination agreements like those discussed in the following section.

In addition, before you interview anyone for a sensitive job, have the applicant sign an interview nondisclosure agreement promising to keep confidential any company trade secrets learned during the interview process and promising not to disclose any trade secrets of a current or former employer. Such an agreement can be found in Chapter 4, Section D.

9. Deal With Departing Employees

The primary source of trade secret leaks is former employees. It is very important to take special precautions when an employee who has signed an NDA decides to leave or is fired.

a. Exit interviews and acknowledgment of obligations form

Before an employee leaves, your company's security officer or other person in charge of the trade secrecy program should conduct an exit interview. Use this opportunity to remind the employee of the obligation not to disclose company trade secrets to others, particularly the new employer. Wherever possible, prepare a list generally describing the specific trade secrets the employee has knowledge of and review it together. Give the employee a copy of the list. Also, remind the employee to return all company documents and materials before leaving. If the employee wants to keep a work sample, make sure it contains no confidential information. Finally, try to find out as much as possible about the worker's new employer and job responsibilities. This will help you determine whether the employee might be tempted to reveal trade secrets to a new employer. If you think this is possible, you may want to send the new employer the letter in Section 9b below.

Give the employee a copy of any nondisclosure and/or noncompetition agreement you and the employee have signed. Go over the agreement and make sure the employee understands the provisions and appreciates that the company is serious about protecting its trade secrets. Finally, ask the employee to sign an acknowledgment of obligations (a sample form is shown below). If the employee refuses to sign, be sure to note that in your personnel files. The refusal may be helpful if you later attempt to obtain a court order to prevent the employee from disclosing company trade secrets.

 The full text of the Acknowledgment of Obligations agreement is on the CD-ROM under the file name Acknowledgment.rtf. See Appendix B for instructions on using the CD-ROM.

Acknowledgment of Obligations

1. I acknowledge that during my employment with Mystery Web Development, Inc. (the Company) I have received or been exposed to trade secrets of the Company including, but not limited to, the following: [*Check applicable boxes*]

❐ Financial data

❐ Price or costing data

❐ Customer and vendor lists

❐ Marketing plans and data

❐ Personnel data

❐ Technical information concerning Company research and development projects, including [*Describe*] _____

❐ Product design and specification data, including [*Describe*] _____

❐ Patent applications and disclosures, including [*Describe*] _____

❐ Product information, including [*Describe*] _____

❐ Other [*Describe*] _____

2. I have read, signed and been furnished with a copy of my [*Choose one*] Employment/Non-disclosure Agreement with the Company. I have complied with and will continue to comply with all of the provisions of the Agreement, including my obligation to preserve as confidential all of the Company's trade secrets.

3. I do not have in my possession original documents, copies of them or any other thing containing Company trade secrets. I have not disclosed Company trade secrets to anyone not authorized by the Company to receive them.

4. I have returned to my supervisor all identification badges, keys and other access devices issued to me by the Company.

Jennifer Jones

Date: 2/15/0X

b. Informing new employers about nondisclosure agreement

If, as a result of your exit interview or for some other reason, you're concerned that a departing employee may reveal company trade secrets to a new employer, consider sending the new employer a polite warning letter. You can let the company know that your ex-employee has signed a nondisclosure agreement and that you are serious about enforcing it. Your letter serves two purposes:

1. It may help deter both the employee and new employer from breaching the nondisclosure agreement.

2. If a breach does occur, it will establish that the new employer knew that the employee possessed your trade secrets and had a duty not to disclose them without your permission. This will make the new employer, along with your ex-employee, liable for any unauthorized disclosure. And if the ex-employee makes an unauthorized disclosure, it will enable you to obtain a court order barring the new employer from using any of your trade secrets. (See Chapter 6.)

Be careful how you write this letter. Don't accuse anyone of trying to steal trade secrets; just stick to the facts. A letter making wild accusations could get your ex-employee fired because the other company fears you might sue. If this occurs, your ex-employee might sue your company for defamation or slander. Also, don't describe the trade secrets involved in detail; a general description of the subject matter is sufficient.

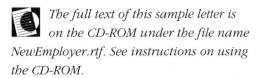 *The full text of this sample letter is on the CD-ROM under the file name NewEmployer.rtf. See instructions on using the CD-ROM.*

Send this letter by certified mail, return receipt requested. A copy should also be sent to the former employee.

July 12, 20XX

To Whom It May Concern:

We understand that Olivia Williams has decided to join your company. We would like to inform you of the following facts:

During her employment by the PineTree Robotics Company, Olivia Williams had access to our trade secrets including, but not limited to, advanced information about robotic visual scanning algorithms.

In connection with her employment, Ms. Williams signed an Employment Agreement in which she promised not to disclose or utilize any of our trade secrets without our permission. The Agreement remains in full force and effect.

At the time Ms. Williams left our company, she was informed of her continuing obligations under the Employment Agreement. She signed an acknowledgment of these obligations, a copy of which is enclosed.

We are confident that Ms. Williams intends to comply with her obligations and respect our trade secrets. We also trust that your company will not assign her to a position that might risk disclosure of our trade secrets.

If you have any questions regarding these matters, we will be happy to clarify them for you. In addition, if at any time you wish to know whether information provided you by Ms. Williams is a trade secret owned by us, we will be happy to work out a procedure for providing you with this information.

Very truly yours,

Jane Matthews

cc: Olivia Williams

Trade Secrets and the Government

Information that is held by the U.S. government may be disclosed upon request of citizens under the Freedom of Information Act (5 U.S.C. § 552). If you disclose trade secret information to the government—for example, your company creates software for government use—how can you prevent further disclosure of those software secrets under the Freedom of Information Act? There is a way the information will not be disclosed if the trade secret documents are clearly marked with the following notice:

This material is subject to exemption under the provisions of the Freedom of Information Act, specifically, 5 U.S.C. § 552(b)(4).

In addition, if you contract with the federal government, any proprietary materials you license or transfer should be marked with a legend that restricts rights. This is particularly important in the case of software. We suggest the following legend, for example, in the case of software licensed to the federal government:

The software is furnished with RESTRICTED RIGHTS. Use, duplication or disclosure is subject to restrictions as set forth in paragraph (b)(3)(B) of the Rights in Technical Data and Computer Software Clause in DAR 7-104.9(a) and in subparagraph (c)(1)(ii) of 252.227-7013; 52.227-19(a) through (d) and applicable ADP Schedule Contract. Unpublished rights are reserved under the copyright laws of the United States. The U.S. Government agrees that any such products licensed which have appropriate RESTRICTED RIGHTS legends applied on them shall be provided only with RESTRICTED RIGHTS. ■

3

Nondisclosure Agreements: The Basics

This chapter explains the elements of a basic NDA and how to create a straightforward agreement. We also discuss how to modify a basic NDA to include provisions that can strengthen your rights and make it easier to resolve disputes, and how to import nondisclosure provisions into an agreement such as a licensing or service contract.

You can use the agreement in this chapter when disclosing secrets to a contractor, a potential investor or a prospective business partner. Go to Chapter 4 if you need a nondisclosure agreement geared to one of these specific situations:

- an employee has access to your company's trade secrets
- another business, with which you're negotiating, may disclose trade secrets
- outsiders who visit your company might learn trade secrets
- prospective employees might learn trade secrets during the interview process
- a company that's considering licensing software you're developing may learn trade secrets
- you're giving software to beta testers

 The agreements in this chapter and in Chapter 4 may be found on the CD-ROM at the back of the book.

You must protect your confidential information. *Although a nondisclosure agreement will assure your right to sue and demonstrates your diligence in protecting secrets, it will not guarantee your success in court. You can never rely solely on an agreement as a basis for protection of confidential information. As explained in Chapter 2, you must also be able to prove that you took reasonable steps to protect your secret and that the secret has not become known to the public.*

Compare before signing. *If you are given an NDA to sign, you can evaluate the agreement by comparing it to the model provisions and reviewing the information in this chapter.*

A. Essential Provisions of an NDA

A nondisclosure agreement should:

- define the trade secrets
- exclude what is not protected as a trade secret
- establish a duty to keep the confidential information secret; and
- state the length of time the agreement will be in force.

A sample NDA is shown below. In subsequent sections we provide alternative versions of many of the provisions in this agreement.

Basic Nondisclosure Agreement

This Nondisclosure Agreement (the "Agreement") is entered into by and between Speculative Ventures, a California corporation with its principal offices at 1282 47th Avenue, San Francisco, California ("Disclosing Party") and Sasha Lorenz, a sole proprietor, located at 412 Mission Street, San Francisco, California ("Receiving Party") for the purpose of preventing the unauthorized disclosure of Confidential Information as defined below. The parties agree to enter into a confidential relationship with respect to the disclosure of certain proprietary and confidential information ("Confidential Information").

1. Definition of Confidential Information. For purposes of this Agreement, "Confidential Information" shall include all information or material that has or could have commercial value or other utility in the business in which Disclosing Party is engaged. If Confidential Information is in written form, the Disclosing Party shall label or stamp the materials with the word "Confidential" or some similar warning. If Confidential Information is transmitted orally, the Disclosing Party shall promptly provide a writing indicating that such oral communication constituted Confidential Information.

2. Exclusions from Confidential Information. Receiving Party's obligations under this Agreement do not extend to information that is: (a) publicly known at the time of disclosure or subsequently becomes publicly known through no fault of the Receiving Party; (b) discovered or created by the Receiving Party before disclosure by Disclosing Party; (c) learned by the Receiving Party through legitimate means other than from the Disclosing Party or Disclosing Party's representatives; or (d) is disclosed by Receiving Party with Disclosing Party's prior written approval.

3. Obligations of Receiving Party. Receiving Party shall hold and maintain the Confidential Information in strictest confidence for the sole and exclusive benefit of the Disclosing Party. Receiving Party shall carefully restrict access to Confidential Information to employees, contractors and third parties as is reasonably required and shall require those persons to sign nondisclosure restrictions at least as protective as those in this Agreement. Receiving Party shall not, without prior written approval of Disclosing Party, use for Receiving Party's own benefit, publish, copy, or otherwise disclose to others, or permit the use by others for their benefit or to the detriment of Disclosing Party, any Confidential Information. Receiving Party shall return to Disclosing Party any and all records, notes, and other written, printed, or tangible materials in its possession pertaining to Confidential Information immediately if Disclosing Party requests it in writing.

4. Time Periods. The nondisclosure provisions of this Agreement shall survive the termination of this Agreement and Receiving Party's duty to hold Confidential Information in confidence shall remain in effect until the Confidential Information no longer qualifies as a trade secret or until Disclosing Party sends Receiving Party written notice releasing Receiving Party from this Agreement, whichever occurs first.

5. Relationships. Nothing contained in this Agreement shall be deemed to constitute either party a partner, joint venturer or employee of the other party for any purpose.

6. Severability. If a court finds any provision of this Agreement invalid or unenforceable, the remainder of this Agreement shall be interpreted so as best to effect the intent of the parties.

7. Integration. This Agreement expresses the complete understanding of the parties with respect to the subject matter and supersedes all prior proposals, agreements, representations and understandings. This Agreement may not be amended except in a writing signed by both parties.

8. Waiver. The failure to exercise any right provided in this Agreement shall not be a waiver of prior or subsequent rights.

This Agreement and each party's obligations shall be binding on the representatives, assigns and successors of such party. Each party has signed this Agreement through its authorized representative.

Donna Maria Ciccone

Donna Maria Ciccone

Date: _____

Sasha Lorenz

Sasha Lorenz

Date: _____

1. Who Is Disclosing? Who Is Receiving?

In the sample agreement, the "Disclosing Party" is the person disclosing secrets, and "Receiving Party" is the person or company who receives the confidential information and is obligated to keep it secret. The terms are capitalized to indicate they are defined within the agreement. The sample agreement is a "one-way" (or in legalese, "unilateral") agreement—that is, only one party is disclosing secrets.

If both sides are disclosing secrets to each other you should modify the agreement to make it a mutual (or "bilateral") nondisclosure agreement. To do that, substitute the following paragraph for the first paragraph in the agreement.

This Nondisclosure agreement (the "Agreement") is entered into by and between ____ [insert your name, business form and address] and ____ [insert name, business form and address of other person or company with whom you are exchanging information] collectively referred to as the "parties" for the purpose of preventing the unauthorized disclosure of Confidential Information as defined below. The parties agree to enter into a confidential relationship with respect to the disclosure by one or each (the "Disclosing Party") to the other (the "Receiving Party") of certain proprietary and confidential information (the "Confidential Information").

---

2. Defining the Trade Secrets

Every nondisclosure agreement defines its trade secrets, often referred to as "confidential information." This definition establishes the subject matter of the disclosure. There are three common approaches to defining confidential information: (1) using a system to mark all confidential information; (2) listing trade secret categories; or (3) specifically identifying the confidential information.

What's best for your company? That depends on your secrets and how you disclose them. If your company is built around one or two secrets—for example, a famous recipe or formula—you can specifically identify the materials. You can also use that approach if you are disclosing one or two secrets to a contractor. If your company focuses on several categories of secret information, for example, computer code, sales information and marketing plans, a list approach will work with employees and contractors. If your company has a wide variety of secrets and is constantly developing new ones, you should specifically identify secrets.

Here's an example of the list approach, taken from the Employee Nondisclosure Agreement in Chapter 4.

EXAMPLE: Definition of Confidential Information

"Confidential Information" means information or material that is commercially valuable to the Disclosing Party and not generally known or readily ascertainable in the industry. This includes, but is not limited to:

(a) technical information concerning the Disclosing Party's products and services, including product know-how, formula, designs, devices, diagrams, software code, test results, processes, inventions, research projects and product development, technical memoranda and correspondence;

(b) information concerning the Disclosing Party's business, including cost information, profits, sales information, accounting and unpublished financial information, business plans, markets and marketing methods, customer lists and customer information, purchasing techniques, supplier lists and supplier information and advertising strategies;

(c) information concerning the Disclosing Party's employees, including salaries, strengths, weaknesses and skills;

(d) information submitted by the Disclosing Party's customers, suppliers, employees, consultants or co-venture partners with the Disclosing Party for study, evaluation or use; and

(e) any other information not generally known to the public that, if misused or disclosed, could reasonably be expected to adversely affect the Disclosing Party's business.

Using a list approach is fine, provided that you can find something on the list that fits your disclosure. For example, if you are disclosing a confidential software program, your nondisclosure agreement should include a category such as "programming code" or "software code" that accurately reflects your secret material. Although the final paragraph in the example, above, includes "any other information," you will be better off not relying solely on this statement. Courts that interpret NDAs often prefer specificity.

If confidential information is fairly specific—for example, a unique method of preparing income tax statements—define it specifically.

EXAMPLE: Definition of Confidential Information

The following constitutes Confidential Information: *business method for preparing income tax statements and related algorithms and software code.*

Another approach to identifying trade secrets is to state that the disclosing party will certify what is and what is not confidential. For example, physical disclosures such as written materials or software will be clearly marked "Confidential." In the case of oral disclosures, the disclosing party provides written confirmation that a trade secret was disclosed. Here is an appropriate provision taken from the sample NDA in the previous section.

EXAMPLE: Definition of Confidential Information

(Written or Oral). For purposes of this Agreement, "Confidential Information" includes all information or material that has or could have commercial value or other utility in the business in which Disclosing Party is engaged. If Confidential Information is in written form, the Disclosing Party shall label or stamp the materials with the word "Confidential" or some similar warning. If Confidential Information is transmitted orally, the Disclosing Party shall promptly provide a writing indicating that such oral communication constituted Confidential Information.

When confirming an oral disclosure, avoid disclosing the content of the trade secret. An email or letter is acceptable, but the parties should keep copies of all such correspondence. A sample letter is shown below.

Letter Confirming Oral Disclosure

Date:

Dear Sam,

Today at lunch, I disclosed information to you about my kaleidoscopic projection system—specifically, the manner in which I have configured and wired the bulbs in the device. That information is confidential (as described in our nondisclosure agreement) and this letter is intended to confirm the disclosure.

William

---

3. Excluding Information That Is Not Confidential

You cannot prohibit the receiving party from disclosing information that is publicly known, legitimately acquired from another source or developed by the receiving party before meeting you. Similarly, it is not unlawful if the receiving party discloses your secret with your permission. These legal exceptions exist with or without an agreement, but they are commonly included in a contract to make it clear to everyone that such information is not considered a trade secret.

EXAMPLE: Exclusions of Confidential Information

Receiving Party's obligations under this Agreement do not extend to information that is: (a) publicly known at the time of disclosure under this Agreement or subsequently becomes publicly known through no fault of the Receiving Party; (b) discovered or created by the Receiving Party prior to disclosure by Disclosing Party; (c) otherwise learned by the Receiving Party through legitimate means other than from the Disclosing Party or Disclosing Party's representatives; or (d) is disclosed by Receiving Party with Disclosing Party's prior written approval.

In some cases, a business presented with your nondisclosure agreement may request the right to exclude information that is independently developed *after* the disclosure. In other words, the business might want to change subsection (b) to read, "(b) discovered or independently created by Receiving Party prior to *or after* disclosure by Disclosing Party."

By making this change, the other company can create new products after exposure to your secret, provided that your secret is not used to develop them. You may wonder how it is possible for a company once exposed to your secret to develop a new product without using that trade secret. One possibility is that one division of a large company could invent something without any contact with the division that has been exposed to your secret. Some

companies even establish clean room methods (see Chapter 1).

Although it is possible for a company to independently develop products or information without using your disclosed secret, we recommend avoiding this modification if possible.

4. Duty to Keep Information Secret

The heart of a nondisclosure agreement is a statement establishing a confidential relationship between the parties. The statement sets out the duty of the Receiving Party to maintain the information in confidence and to limit its use. Often, this duty is established by one sentence: "The Receiving Party shall hold and maintain the Confidential Information of the other party in strictest confidence for the sole and exclusive benefit of the Disclosing Party." In other cases, the provision may be more detailed and may include obligations to return information. A detailed provision is provided below.

The simpler provision is usually suitable when entering into an NDA with an individual such as an independent contractor. Use the more detailed one if your secrets may be used by more than one individual within a business. The detailed provision provides that the receiving party has to restrict access to persons within the company who are also bound by this agreement.

EXAMPLE: Provision Establishing a Duty of Nondisclosure

Receiving Party shall hold and maintain the Confidential Information of the Disclosing Party in strictest confidence for the sole and exclusive benefit of the Disclosing Party. Receiving Party shall carefully restrict access to Confidential Information to employees, contractors and third parties as is reasonably required and only to persons subject to nondisclosure restrictions at least as protective as those set forth in this Agreement. Receiving Party shall not, without prior written approval of Disclosing Party, use for Receiving Party's own benefit, publish, copy, or otherwise disclose to others, or permit the use by others for their benefit or to the detriment of Disclosing Party, any Confidential Information.

In some cases, you may want to impose additional requirements. For example, the Prospective Software Licensee Nondisclosure Agreement in Chapter 4 contains a prohibition against reverse engineering, decompiling or disassembling the software. This prohibits the receiving party (the user of licensed software) from learning more about the trade secrets.

You may also insist on the return of all trade secret materials that you furnished under the agreement. In that case, add the following language to the receiving party's obligations.

EXAMPLE: Return of Materials

Receiving Party shall return to Disclosing Party any and all records, notes, and other written, printed, or tangible materials in its possession pertaining to Confidential Information immediately if Disclosing Party requests it in writing.

5. Duration of the Agreement

How long does the duty of confidentiality last? The sample agreement offers three alternative approaches: an indefinite period that terminates when the information is no longer a trade secret; a fixed period of time; or a combination of the two.

EXAMPLE: Unlimited Time Period

This Agreement and Receiving Party's duty to hold Disclosing Party's Confidential Information in confidence shall remain in effect until the Confidential Information no longer qualifies as a trade secret or until Disclosing Party sends Receiving Party written notice releasing Receiving Party from this Agreement, whichever occurs first.

EXAMPLE: Fixed Time Period

This Agreement and Receiving Party's duty to hold Disclosing Party's Confidential Information in confidence shall remain in effect until _____.

EXAMPLE: Fixed Time Period With Exceptions

This Agreement and Receiving Party's duty to hold Disclosing Party's Confidential Information in confidence shall remain in effect until _____ or until one of the following occurs:

(a) the Disclosing Party sends the Receiving Party written notice releasing it from this Agreement, or

(b) the information disclosed under this Agreement ceases to be a trade secret.

The time period is often an issue of negotiation. You, as the disclosing party, will usually want an open period with no limits; receiving parties want a short period. For employee and contractor agreements, the term is often unlimited or ends only when the trade secret becomes public knowledge. Five years is a common length in nondisclosure agreements that involve business negotiations and product submissions although many companies insist on two or three years.

We recommend that you seek as long a time as possible, preferably unlimited. But realize that some businesses want a fixed period of time and some courts, when interpreting NDAs, require that the time period be reasonable. Determining "reasonableness" is subjective and depends on the confidential material and the nature of the industry. For example, some trade secrets within the software or Internet industries may be short-lived. Other trade secrets—

for example, the Coca-Cola formula—have been preserved as a secret for over a century. If it is likely, for example, that others will stumble upon the same secret or innovation or that it will be reverse engineered within a few years, then you are unlikely to be damaged by a two- or three-year period. Keep in mind that once the time period is over, the disclosing party is free to reveal your secrets.

6. Miscellaneous Provisions

The sample NDA includes four miscellaneous provisions. These standard provisions (sometimes known as "boilerplate") are included at the end of most contracts. They actually have little in common with one another except for the fact that they don't fit anywhere else in the agreement. They're contract orphans. Still, these provisions are very important and can affect how disputes are resolved and how a court enforces the contract.

Relationships. Your relationship with the receiving party is usually defined by the agreement that you are signing—for example an employment, licensing or investment agreement. To an outsider, it may appear that you have a different relationship, such as a partnership or joint venture. It's possible that an unscrupulous business will try to capitalize on this appearance and make a third-party deal. That is, the receiving party may claim to be your partner to obtain a benefit from a distributor or sublicensee. To avoid liability for such a situation, most agreements include a provision like this one, disclaiming any relationship other than that defined in the agreement. We recommend that you include such a provision and take care to tailor it to the agreement. For example, if you are using it in an employment agreement, you would delete the reference to employees. If you are using it in a partnership agreement, take out the reference to partners, and so forth.

EXAMPLE: Relationships
Nothing contained in this Agreement shall be deemed to constitute either party a partner, joint venturer or employee of the other party for any purpose.

Severability. The severability clause provides that if you wind up in a lawsuit over the agreement and a court rules that one part of the agreement is invalid, that part can be cut out and the rest of the agreement will remain valid. If you don't include a severability clause and some portion of your agreement is deemed invalid, then the whole agreement may be canceled.

EXAMPLE: Severability.
If a court finds any provision of this Agreement invalid or unenforceable, the remainder of this Agreement shall be interpreted so as best to effect the intent of the parties.

Integration. In the process of negotiation and contract drafting, you and the other party may make many oral or written statements. Some of these statements make it into the final agreement. Others don't. The integration provision verifies that the version you are signing is the final version, and that neither of you can rely on statements made in the past. *This is it!* Without an integration provision, it's possible that either party could claim rights based upon promises made before the deal was signed.

A second function of the integration provision is to establish that if any party makes promises after the agreement is signed, those promises will be binding only if they are made in a signed amendment (addendum) to the agreement.

EXAMPLE: Integration
This Agreement expresses the complete understanding of the parties with respect to the subject matter and supersedes all prior proposals, agreements, representations and understandings. This Agreement may not be amended except in a writing signed by both parties.

Watch Out for "We'll Fix It Later" Promises. *The integration clause closes the door on any oral or written promises. Don't sign an agreement if something is missing and don't accept an assurance that the other party will correct it later.*

Waiver. This provision states that even if you don't promptly complain about a violation of the NDA, you still have the right to complain about it later. Without this kind of clause, if you know the other party has breached the agreement but you let it pass, you give up (waive) your right to sue over it. For example, imagine that the receiving party is supposed to use the secret information in two products but not in a third. You're aware that the receiving party is violating the agreement, but you are willing to permit it because you are being paid more money and don't have a competing product. After several years, however, you no longer want to permit the use of the secret in the third product. A waiver provision makes it possible for you to sue. The receiving party cannot defend itself by claiming it relied on your past practice of accepting its breaches. Of course, the provision swings both ways. If you breach the agreement, you cannot rely on the other party's past acceptance of *your* behavior.

> **EXAMPLE: Waiver**
> The failure to exercise any right provided in this Agreement shall not be a waiver of prior or subsequent rights.

7. Signatures

The parties don't have to be in the same room when they sign the agreement. It's even fine if the dates are a few days apart. Each party should sign two copies, and keep one. This way, both parties have an original signed agreement.

a. Who is authorized to sign

Someone with the necessary authority must sign the agreement on behalf of each party. To reinforce this, you will note that the sample agreement states that: "Each party has signed this Agreement through its authorized representative."

Use the following rules to determine the proper signature line:

Sole Proprietorship. If you are a sole proprietorship, simply sign your own name. If the receiving party is a married couple doing business as a sole proprietorship, both should sign the NDA. On the other hand, if the disclosing party is a married couple doing business as a sole proprietorship, only the party under whom the sole proprietorship is registered (with the state or county clerk) needs to sign. If the sole proprietorship has a fictitious business name (sometimes known as a *dba*), insert it above the signature line. For example, if Tom Stein is a sole proprietor doing business as Lukie Boy Inventions, Tom would sign an NDA as follows:

> ## Lukie Boy Inventions
>
> By: _____
>
> Tom Stein, sole proprietor

Partnership. When a general or limited partnership enters into an agreement, the only person authorized to sign the agreement is a general partner or someone who has written authority (usually in the form of a partnership resolution) from a general partner. The name of the partnership must be mentioned above the signature line or the partnership will not be bound (only the person signing the agreement will be bound). For example, say Cindy Barrett were a general partner in Reality Manufacturing Partnership. She would sign as follows:

Reality Manufacturing Partnership

By: _____

Cindy Barrett, general partner

Corporation or LLC. To bind a corporation or limited liability company (LLC), only a person authorized by the business can sign the agreement. The president or chief executive officer (CEO) usually has such power but not every executive of a corporation or every member of an LLC has this authority. If in doubt, ask for written proof of the authority. This proof is usually in the form of a corporate resolution or the operating agreement of an LLC. Put the name of the corporation or LLC above the signature line; otherwise, the corporation may not be bound (only the person signing the agreement will be bound). For example, Karen Foley, CEO of Insincere Marketing, would sign as follows:

Insincere Marketing, Inc., a New York corporation

By: _____

Karen Foley, CEO

If you have doubts about the person's credibility, don't proceed until you are satisfied that the person has full authority to represent the company.

b. Faxed or electronic signatures

It's okay to use a faxed signature if both parties accept its authenticity. If one party claims a forgery, it may be difficult to prove a signature's authenticity from the fax alone. So if you fax the signed agreement follow up by mailing or overnighting the signed original.

Although "electronic signatures" are now valid under federal law, we recommend relying on paper agreements and traditional signatures for the time being. Under this law (the Electronic Signatures in Global and International Commerce Act), an electronic contract is an agreement created and "signed" in electronic form—in other words, no paper copies are used. For example, you could write a nondisclosure agreement on your computer and email it to a business associate, who emails it back with an electronic signature indicating acceptance. But secure methods of electronic signatures have not yet been popularized, so stick with paper for now.

B. Additional Contract Provisions

Here are some other provisions that you can add to your agreement. These provisions are not essential but we recommend including at least some of them if you have sufficient bargaining power. They can give you additional rights and create additional obligations on the other party.

1. Injunctive Relief

An injunction is a court order directing a person to do (or stop doing) something. If someone violated your NDA, you would want a court order directing that person to stop using your secrets. To get an injunction, you must demonstrate to the court that you have suffered or will suffer irreparable harm as a result of the unauthorized use of your secrets. Irreparable harm is harm that can't be compensated for later by money.

Proving that in court is expensive and time-consuming. In order to cut through some of that legal work, some nondisclosure agreements include a provision similar to the one below. In it, the receiving party agrees that the harm caused by a breach is irreparable, so you will have less to prove if and when you seek a court order. This provision only makes it easier to obtain an injunction; by itself, it will not compel a judge to order an injunction. In other words, don't expect that a judge will automatically stop the disclosure simply because this provision is in your agreement. To get an injunction, you will always need to demonstrate that you are likely to prevail in your dispute. That said, this clause provides some tactical advantages and it's a good idea to include it.

EXAMPLE: Injunctive Relief
Receiving Party acknowledges that any misappropriation of any of the Confidential Information in violation of this Agreement may cause Disclosing Party irreparable harm, the amount of which may be difficult to ascertain, and therefore agrees that the Disclosing Party shall have the right to apply to a court of competent jurisdiction for an order enjoining any such further misappropriation and for such other relief as the Disclosing Party deems appropriate. This right of Disclosing Party is to be in addition to the remedies otherwise available to Disclosing Party.

2. Indemnity

Some NDAs require the receiving party to pay for all damages (lost profits, attorney fees or other expenses) incurred by the other party as a result of the receiving party's breach of the nondisclosure agreement. This obligation is known as indemnification. Leaving out the indemnity provision does not prevent you from suing and collecting damages for a breach (contract law holds the receiving party responsible for a breach), but the clause makes it easier to claim damages. To include indemnity in your nondisclosure agreement, add the following language at the end of the obligations section:

> **EXAMPLE: Indemnity**
> Receiving Party agrees to indemnify the Disclosing Party against any and all losses, damages, claims or expenses incurred or suffered by the Disclosing Party as a result of the Receiving Party's breach of this Agreement.

3. Attorney Fees

What if the other party breaches the NDA, and you are forced to sue? The rate for business lawyers is $200 to $400 an hour. The filing and initial stages of a lawsuit cost $5,000 to $50,000 and can quickly escalate to more than $100,000, depending on the length of the suit and the subject matter. The amount you pay lawyers could quickly overshadow any amount you might win.

In the United States (unlike many other countries), the loser of a lawsuit is not required to pay the winner's attorney fees. In other words, each party has to pay its own lawyer, regardless of the outcome of the suit. There are two exceptions to this rule:

1) a court may award fees if a specific law permits it; and
2) a court must award attorney fees if a contract provides for it.

If you don't include an attorney fees clause in your agreement, a judge may (in most states) order the award of attorney fees in cases where the theft of the trade secret was willful and malicious. It's up to the judge, which makes things unpredictable. You are far better off using an attorney fees provision like the one below. Because lawyers are so expensive, having an attorney fee provision—that is, having each side afraid it will get stuck paying someone's attorney fees—can prove crucial to ending a dispute.

However, don't be surprised if the other party is opposed to the idea. Why? Because it is the receiving party that is usually sued, not vice-versa, and the receiving party may believe that the provision will encourage you to sue.

> **EXAMPLE: Attorney Fees and Expenses**
> In a dispute arising out of or related to this Agreement, the prevailing party shall have the right to collect from the other party its reasonable attorney fees and costs and necessary expenditures.

This attorney fees provision is mutual—that is, whoever wins the lawsuit is awarded attorney fees. This is fair, and encourages the quick resolution of lawsuits. We discourage a provision that allows only one party to receive attorney fees. No matter which side they favor, such provisions create an uneven playing field for resolving disputes. One state (California) recognizes this unfairness and automatically converts a one-way attorney fees contract provision into a mutual one.

4. Arbitration and Mediation

Arbitration and mediation are referred to as alternative dispute resolution (ADR) procedures because they offer ways to end squabbles without litigation. These ADR procedures have become popular over the last decade because they avoid the court system and can save time and money. However, taking a dispute out of the court system may not always be the right decision, because you may be bound by a decision from which there is no means of appeal. Below we discuss both options and offer examples of appropriate contract provisions.

a. Arbitration

Arbitration is like going to court with less formality and expense. Instead of filing a lawsuit, the parties hire one or more arbitrators to evaluate the dispute and make a determination. The arbitration process can be relatively simple; usually arbitration involves some document preparation and a hearing. A lawyer is not required to arbitrate, but many parties use attorneys for help in presenting the strongest legal arguments.

The arbitrator's determination may be advisory (in which case either party can disregard it and file a lawsuit) or it may be binding. A binding decision can be enforced by a court and cannot be overturned unless something especially unfair happened—for example, the arbitrator ruled against you and you later learn that the arbitrator owned stock in your opponent's company.

In order to arbitrate a dispute, both parties must consent. Unfortunately, when you are in the midst of a dispute, it's hard to get the parties to agree to anything. So, the best method of guaranteeing arbitration is to include an arbitration provision in your nondisclosure agreement.

Arbitration is not, however, always preferable to litigation. Even though ADR is quicker than going through a trial, it may take several weeks to initiate ADR proceedings. By going to court, however, a business may obtain a temporary court order restraining disclosure (TRO) in less time than it takes to initiate arbitration. This initial period of the dispute can be crucial when you're concerned about the loss of secrecy. For this reason, you need to weigh the potential cost of litigation versus the speed of obtaining relief. For a small company with limited resources, arbitration is usually the preferable route.

Many businesses are opposed to arbitration for other reasons as well. They may have recently lost an arbitration proceeding and refuse to participate in another one. They may be fearful that the dispute will be placed in the hands of an inappropriate arbitrator or they may prefer the litigation process in order to intimidate the other party. In addition, some arbitrations can be expensive and end up being appealed in the court system.

Arbitration at a Glance

It's less expensive than a lawsuit.

Arbitration can be completed within several months. Litigation can continue for several years.

You can hire an arbitrator with technical knowledge—for example, about patents—if necessary.

There is no right to discovery (the process by which the parties must disclose information about their cases) unless you require it in your arbitration provision.

It may be possible to obtain immediate relief quicker by going to court.

There is no appeal of a binding arbitration ruling. It can be set aside only if you can prove that the arbitrator was biased or that the ruling violated public policy.

You must pay the arbitrators; the fees are often $10,000 or more.

Lawyers are usually necessary, though their fees will probably be lower than if you sued in court.

Many associations and companies offer private arbitration: the most well-known organization is the American Arbitration Association (AAA). If your dispute relates to patents as well as trade secrets, the AAA has special Patent Arbitration Rules and a national panel of patent arbitrators. The AAA has offices in every state and can provide mediators and arbitrators in most areas. If you would like to check the availability of AAA arbitrators or mediators in your area before using one of these clauses, visit www.adr.org.

If you would like to use arbitration, we suggest the following provision. The statement at the end of the provision ("An award of arbitration may be confirmed in a court of competent jurisdiction") means that the winner can convert the arbitration into a court judgment. That way, a court can order the loser to pay damages or abide by the decision.

In the next section we provide a mediation clause that offers arbitration as a back-up option, to be used if mediation fails.

EXAMPLE: Arbitration

If a dispute arises under or relating to this Agreement, the parties agree to submit the dispute to binding arbitration in the state of ___ *[insert state in which parties agree to arbitrate]* or another location mutually agreeable to the parties. The arbitration shall be conducted on a confidential basis pursuant to the Commercial Arbitration Rules of the American Arbitration Association. Any decision or award as a result of any such arbitration proceeding shall be in writing and shall provide an explanation for all conclusions of law and fact and shall include the assessment of costs, expenses and reasonable attorney fees. Any such arbitration shall be conducted by an arbitrator experienced in ___*[insert industry experience required for* *arbitrator]* and ____ *[insert area of law that is at the subject of your dispute, for example, licensing law]* law and shall include a written record of the arbitration hearing. The parties reserve the right to object to any individual who is employed by or affiliated with a competing organization or entity. An award of arbitration may be confirmed in a court of competent jurisdiction.

b. Mediation

In mediation, a neutral evaluator (the mediator) attempts to help the parties reach a resolution of their dispute. Both sides sit down with the mediator and tell their stories. The mediator advises ways to resolve the dispute, and the two parties try to agree. If they do, they sign an enforceable settlement agreement. Because it is not binding and because it is less expensive than litigation or arbitration, some businesses prefer mediation, at least as a first step. You can locate a mediator through the American Arbitration Association (www.adr.org) or local bar associations.

Mediation is the most inexpensive and peaceable method of solving problems. You can arrive at a settlement rather than being told how to resolve the dispute by an arbitrator or judge. It's less likely to exacerbate bad feelings between the parties, as lawsuits inevitably do.

By itself, however, mediation is often not enough because it doesn't force the parties to end the dispute. If you cannot resolve the dispute with mediation, you must find some binding method of ending the battle, either arbitration or litigation. Sometimes one party chooses mediation simply to buy more time. Keep in mind, as we mentioned in the preceding section, that time is generally of the essence in disputes over the disclosure of information.

If you want to use a mediation clause, we suggest a provision like the one below, which progresses from informal meeting to mediation and then to arbitration.

> **EXAMPLE: Mediation & Arbitration**
> The parties agree that any dispute or difference between them arising under this Agreement shall be settled first by a meeting of the parties attempting to confer and resolve the dispute in a good faith manner.
>
> If the parties cannot resolve their dispute after conferring, any party may require the other to submit the matter to non-binding mediation, utilizing the services of an impartial professional mediator approved by both parties.
>
> If the parties cannot come to an agreement following mediation, they will submit the matter to binding arbitration at a location mutually agreeable to the parties. The arbitration shall be conducted on a confidential basis under the Commercial Arbitration Rules of the American Arbitration Association. Any decision or award as a result of any such arbitration proceeding shall include the assessment of costs, expenses and reasonable attorney

fees and shall include a written record of the proceedings and a written determination of the arbitrators. Absent an agreement to the contrary, any such arbitration shall be conducted by an arbitrator experienced in intellectual property law. The parties may object to any individual who is employed by or affiliated with a competing organization or entity. In the event of any such dispute or difference, either party may give to the other notice requiring that the matter be settled by arbitration. An award of arbitration shall be final and binding on the parties and may be confirmed in a court of competent jurisdiction.

Nolo's How to Mediate Your Dispute: Find a Solution Quickly and Cheaply Outside the Courtroom, *by Peter Lovenheim provides more information on mediation and arbitration.*

5. Which State's Law Will Govern Disputes

Every state has laws regarding contract interpretation and trade secrecy. You can choose any state's laws to govern the agreement, regardless of where you live or where the agreement is signed. Most businesses favor the state where their headquarters are located.

Does it matter which state you choose? Some states have a reputation of being favorable for certain kinds of disputes. For example, California's state and federal courts have resolved many high-tech dis-

putes; as a body of law has developed, judges' decisions have become more predictable. Generally, however, the differences in state law are not great enough to make this a major negotiating issue.

EXAMPLE: Governing Law
This Agreement shall be governed in accordance with the laws of the State of
_____.

Don't confuse jurisdiction and governing law. *Selecting where a dispute will be settled, described below, is more important than selecting which state's laws will apply. Sometimes these two provisions are grouped in one paragraph, so read them carefully.*

6. Choosing Jurisdiction

Jurisdiction (sometimes referred to as personal jurisdiction) is the power of a court to bind you by its decision. If a court doesn't have this authority over you, any judgment it issues isn't worth anything. A court can get jurisdiction over you in three ways: (1) you are a resident of the state in which the court is located; (2) you have sufficient contacts in the state, such as selling considerable merchandise there; or (3) you consent to jurisdiction.

The purpose of adding a jurisdiction provision to an NDA is to get each party to consent in advance to jurisdiction in one county or state and to give up the right to sue or be sued anywhere else. Consider the couple who opened a Burger King franchise in Florida. In their agreement with Burger King, they consented to jurisdiction in Michigan. Later, when problems arose, the couple argued that it wasn't fair to have to travel to Michigan and that they had not understood this provision. The courts upheld the jurisdiction clause and the couple was forced to fight Burger King in a Michigan court.

This may seem like a trivial issue at the time you are negotiating an agreement, but it will be a major issue if there is ever a dispute. In fact, the prospect of hiring lawyers and traveling to another state is often enough to dissuade companies from pursuing a lawsuit. We recommend the following strategies:

- If you have sufficient bargaining power, obtain jurisdiction in your home county.
- If you cannot obtain jurisdiction in your home county, don't say anything about jurisdiction. If there is no reference to jurisdiction, the location of the case is usually determined by whoever files the lawsuit.
- If you *do* include a jurisdiction clause it may be helpful to choose the same state you chose for governing law, as discussed above. It's simpler and more efficient for a court to apply the familiar laws of its own state.

EXAMPLE: Jurisdiction
The parties consent to the exclusive jurisdiction and venue of the federal and state courts located in ____ [*insert county and state in which parties agree to litigate*] in any action arising out of or relating to this Agreement. The parties waive any other jurisdiction to which either party might be entitled by domicile or otherwise.

 In some states, jurisdiction clauses are invalid. *Idaho, Montana and Alabama refuse to honor jurisdiction provisions in contracts. In those states, if you use a jurisdiction provision, it will be invalid. The states' reasoning? They think jurisdiction should be determined by law, not by people shopping around for the most convenient or advantageous forum.*

7. Successors and Assigns

It's possible that either may be succeeded by someone else. For example, a sole proprietor's heirs may inherit the business. In that case you would make want to sure that the heirs were bound by the same nondisclosure requirements.

In other cases, a party may assign its rights to another company. For example, the business you sign an NDA with may be acquired by another company—maybe even a competitor of yours. So, if you have the bargaining power, prohibit any assignment of your contract unless you give written consent. But understand that in today's world of acquisitions and mergers, many companies want the freedom to assign agreements and oppose a complete prohibition on assignments.

EXAMPLE: Successors & Assigns

This Agreement shall bind each party's heirs, successors and assigns. Disclosing Party may assign this Agreement to any party at any time. Receiving Party shall not assign any of its rights or obligations under this Agreement without Company's prior written consent. Any assignment or transfer in violation of this section shall be void.

If the other party is concerned that this language gives you too much control, you can soften the effect by agreeing to withhold consent only if you have a valid business reason. What's a valid reason? Perhaps the potential assignee has a poor reputation for maintaining trade secrets, or maybe it is in poor financial shape. You cannot, however, withhold consent for an arbitrary reason, such as that someone from the company once treated you rudely.

EXAMPLE: Assignability—Consent Not Unreasonably Withheld

This Agreement shall bind each party's heirs, successors and assigns. Receiving Party may not assign or transfer its rights or obligations pursuant to this Agreement without the prior written consent of Disclosing Party. Such consent shall not be unreasonably withheld. Any assignment or transfer in violation of this section shall be void.

If you don't have much bargaining power and the other party wants freedom to transfer to affiliates or new owners, you can use a provision such as the one below.

EXAMPLE: Assignability—Consent Not Needed for Affiliates Or New Owners

This Agreement shall bind each party's heirs, successors and assigns. Receiving Party may not assign or transfer its rights or obligations pursuant to this Agreement without the prior written consent of Disclosing Party. However, no consent is required for an assignment or transfer that occurs: (a) to an entity in which Receiving Party owns more than fifty percent of the assets; or (b) as part of a transfer of all or substantially all of the assets of Receiving Party to any party. Any assignment or transfer in violation of this Section shall be void.

C. One NDA or Many?

When you are disclosing information to a company and you are concerned about dissemination within the company you have two choices. You can have everyone who will have access to your trade secrets sign your nondisclosure agreement or you can have an executive or officer of the company sign it and include a requirement that all of the company's employees and contractors who are exposed to the trade secrets be bound by similar agreements.

If each person exposed to the information signs your agreement, you can sue each person individually in the event of a breach. This option is better suited for small entities such as sole proprietorships or a partnership—business forms in which each signatory can be individually liable. The second option is better for larger businesses that operate as corporations or LLCs and are usually only liable as a corporate entity. You can sue only the company for breaking its promise not to disclose; you cannot sue the individual who disclosed the information. It is the one used in the sample agreement with this language.

"Receiving Party shall carefully restrict access to Confidential Information to employees, contractors and third parties as is reasonably required and shall require those persons to sign nondisclosure restrictions at least as protective as those in this Agreement."

D. Adding Nondisclosure Provisions to an Existing Agreement

Instead of creating an NDA from scratch, you may wish to include nondisclosure requirements in a form agreement that you use regularly in your business. An entire nondisclosure agreement can be compressed into one provision, which you can insert in any agreement under which trade secrets will be disclosed. For example, you can insert the provision below into a license, option or service contract.

EXAMPLE: Confidentiality Provision
(a) Confidential Information. The parties acknowledge that each may receive or have access to confidential information (the "Confidential Information"). For purposes of this Agreement, "Confidential Information" shall include all information or material that has or could have commercial value or other utility in the business in which the party part disclosing the information ("Disclosing Party") is engaged. In the event that Confidential Information is in written form, Disclosing Party shall label or stamp the materials with the word "Confidential" or some similar warning. In the event that Confidential Information is transmitted orally, the Disclosing Party shall promptly provide a writing indicating that such oral communication constituted Confidential Information.

(b) Exclusions from Confidential Information. The party receiving the Confidential Information ("Receiving Party) shall not be obligated to preserve the confidentiality of any information that is: (a) publicly known at the time of disclosure under this Agreement or subsequently becomes publicly known through no fault of Receiving Party; (b) discovered or created by Receiving Party prior to the time of disclosure by Disclosing Party; or (c) otherwise learned by Receiving Party through legitimate means other than from

Disclosing Party or anyone connected with Disclosing Party.

(c) Obligations of Receiving Party. Receiving Party shall hold and maintain the Confidential Information of the other party in strictest confidence for the sole and exclusive benefit of Disclosing Party. Receiving Party shall carefully restrict access to any such Confidential Information to persons bound by this Agreement, only on a need-to-know basis. Receiving Party shall not, without prior written approval of Disclosing Party, use for Receiving Party's own benefit, publish, copy, or otherwise disclose to others, or permit the use by others for their benefit or to the detriment of Disclosing Party, any of the Confidential Information. The Receiving Party shall return to Disclosing Party any and all records, notes, and other written, printed, or tangible materials in its

possession pertaining to the Confidential Information immediately on the written request of Disclosing Party.

(d) Time Period. This Agreement and Receiving Party's duty to hold Disclosing Party's Confidential Information in confidence shall remain in effect until [*include year*].

(e) Survival. The nondisclosure provisions of this Agreement shall survive the termination of any relationship between Disclosing Party and Receiving Party.

You can modify this provision to define trade secrets specifically as in Section A2 or to make the time period unlimited, as explained in Section A5. It is possible to augment these provisions to provide even stronger protections; see Section B. ■

Nondisclosure Agreements for Specific Situations

This chapter contains eight nondisclosure agreements specially tailored for common situations. Where applicable, use them instead of the general agreement in Chapter 3. They include agreements to use when you:

- disclose trade secrets to employees
- engage in business negotiations that may reveal trade secrets
- allow outsiders to visit your office, plant or other facility that contains trade secrets
- interview a prospective employee
- give an unfinished software product to a software beta tester
- give a finished software product to a prospective licensee or other customer for evaluation
- allow a research student access to trade secrets, or
- license a customer list or mailing list.

The rest of the chapter contains instructions for creating these agreements, which can be found on the CD-ROM included with the book.

A. Employee Nondisclosure Agreement

The sole purpose of this nondisclosure agreement is to make clear to an employee that he or she may not disclose your trade secrets without permission. We recommend that a new employee sign this agreement prior to starting work. If the agreement is with a current employee, we recommend that you give the employee something of value over and above normal salary and benefits. (See Section A1.)

If you wish, you can include the language of this agreement in an all-encompassing employment agreement covering such additional issues as salary and duties. You may also want to require that if the employee creates anything on the job, it belongs to your company. Chapter 5 contains provisions you can add to this agreement to make sure you own any trade secrets developed by the employee.

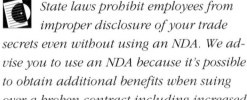 *State laws prohibit employees from improper disclosure of your trade secrets even without using an NDA. We advise you to use an NDA because it's possible to obtain additional benefits when suing over a broken contract including increased damages, payment of attorney fees and a guarantee as to where or how the dispute will be resolved. (See Chapter 6.)*

 This agreement may be found on the CD-ROM at the back of the book under the file name: EmplNondisclose.rtf.

Employee Nondisclosure Agreement

This agreement (the "Agreement") is entered into by _____
("Company") and _____ ("Employee").

[Alternative 1]
In consideration of the commencement of Employee's employment with Company and the compensation that will be paid, Employee and Company agree as follows:

[Alternative 2]
In consideration of Employee's continued employment with Company and also in consideration of:

[Choose one]
❏ the amount of $ _____

❏ options to purchase _____ shares of Company's stock

❏ _____

the receipt and sufficiency of which is acknowledged, the parties agree as follows:

1. Company's Trade Secrets

In the performance of Employee's job duties with Company, Employee will be exposed to Company's Confidential Information. "Confidential Information" means information or material that is commercially valuable to Company and not generally known or readily ascertainable in the industry. This includes, but is not limited to:

(a) technical information concerning Company's products and services, including product know-how, formulas, designs, devices, diagrams, software code, test results, processes, inventions, research projects and product development, technical memoranda and correspondence;

(b) information concerning Company's business, including cost information, profits, sales information, accounting and unpublished financial information, business plans, markets and marketing methods, customer lists and customer information, purchasing techniques, supplier lists and supplier information and advertising strategies;

(c) information concerning Company's employees, including salaries, strengths, weaknesses and skills;

(d) information submitted by Company's customers, suppliers, employees, consultants or co-venture partners with Company for study, evaluation or use; and

(e) any other information not generally known to the public which, if misused or disclosed, could reasonably be expected to adversely affect Company's business.

2. Nondisclosure of Trade Secrets

Employee shall keep Company's Confidential Information, whether or not prepared or developed by Employee, in the strictest confidence. Employee will not disclose such information to anyone outside Company without Company's prior written consent. Nor will Employee make use of any Confidential Information for Employee's own purposes or the benefit of anyone other than Company.

However, Employee shall have no obligation to treat as confidential any information which:

(a) was in Employee's possession or known to Employee, without an obligation to keep it confidential, before such information was disclosed to Employee by Company;

(b) is or becomes public knowledge through a source other than Employee and through no fault of Employee; or

(c) is or becomes lawfully available to Employee from a source other than Company.

3. Confidential Information of Others

Employee will not disclose to Company, use in Company's business, or cause Company to use, any trade secret of others.

4. Return of Materials

When Employee's employment with Company ends, for whatever reason, Employee will promptly deliver to Company all originals and copies of all documents, records, software programs, media and other materials containing any Confidential Information. Employee will also return to Company all equipment, files, software programs and other personal property belonging to Company.

5. Confidentiality Obligation Survives Employment

Employee's obligation to maintain the confidentiality and security of Confidential Information remains even after Employee's employment with Company ends and continues for so long as such Confidential Information remains a trade secret.

6. General Provisions

(a) Relationships: Nothing contained in this Agreement shall be deemed to make Employee a partner or joint venturer of Company for any purpose.

(b) Severability: If a court finds any provision of this Agreement invalid or unenforceable, the remainder of this Agreement shall be interpreted so as best to effect the intent of Company and Employee.

(c) Integration: This Agreement expresses the complete understanding of the parties with respect to the subject matter and supersedes all prior proposals, agreements, representations and understandings. This Agreement may not be amended except in a writing signed by both Company and Employee.

(d) Waiver: The failure to exercise any right provided in this Agreement shall not be a waiver of prior or subsequent rights.

(e) Injunctive Relief: Any misappropriation of any of the Confidential Information in violation of this Agreement may cause Company irreparable harm, the amount of which may be difficult to ascertain, and therefore Employee agrees that Company shall have the right to apply to a court of competent jurisdiction for an order enjoining any such further misappropriation and for such other relief as Company deems appropriate. This right is to be in addition to the remedies otherwise available to Company.

(f) Indemnity: Employee agrees to indemnify Company against any and all losses, damages, claims or expenses incurred or suffered by Company as a result of Employee's breach of this Agreement.

(g) Attorney Fees and Expenses: In a dispute arising out of or related to this Agreement, the prevailing party shall have the right to collect from the other party its reasonable attorney fees and costs and necessary expenditures.

(h) Governing Law. This Agreement shall be governed in accordance with the laws of the State of _____.

(i) Jurisdiction. Employee consents to the exclusive jurisdiction and venue of the federal and state courts located in _____ [*insert county and state in which parties agree to litigate*] in any action arising out of or relating to this Agreement. Employee waives any other venue to which Employee might be entitled by domicile or otherwise.

(j) Successors & Assigns. This Agreement shall bind each party's heirs, successors and assigns. Company may assign this Agreement to any party at any time. Employee shall not assign any of his or her rights or obligations under this Agreement without Company's prior written consent. Any assignment or transfer in violation of this section shall be void.

7. Signatures

Employee has carefully read all of this Agreement and agrees that all of the restrictions set forth are fair and reasonably required to protect Company's interests. Employee has received a copy of this Agreement as signed by the parties.

Employee:

_____

(Signature)

_____

(Typed or Printed Name)

Date:_____

Company:

_____

(Signature)

_____

(Typed or Printed Name)

Date: _____

1. Introductory Paragraph

Fill in the name of the company and employee.

Select Alternative 1 if a new employee will be signing the agreement.

Select Alternative 2 if the agreement is with a current employee. To ensure that the agreement will be legally binding, the employee should receive something of value over and above normal salary and benefits for signing it—for example, cash, additional vacation time, stock options or other benefits. Specify the compensation to be provided. It does not have to be substantial—for example, several additional days of vacation per year should do it.

2. Company's Trade Secrets

This clause defines your company's trade secrets. You don't need to add anything to it; it sets out the types of information and material that should be considered trade secrets. There are several ways to define your company's trade secrets; you can use any of the alternatives provided in Chapter 3, Section A2.

3. Nondisclosure of Trade Secrets

This clause bars the employee from making unauthorized disclosures of your trade secrets. It also requires the employee to protect the trade secrets and shows that you're serious about keeping trade secrets secret.

This clause also explains that the employee's nondisclosure obligation does not extend to:

- information the employee knew before coming to work for the company
- information learned from sources outside the company, or
- information that is public knowledge (so long as the employee didn't make it public).

4. Confidential Information of Others

It is a good idea to remind new employees not to disclose to the company trade secrets learned from prior employers or others. Employers who take advantage of such information can easily end up being sued.

5. Return of Materials

This clause requires employees to return all materials containing trade secrets when they leave the company. They should be reminded of this obligation before they leave. (See Chapter 2 for suggestions on conducting an "exit interview" when an employee leaves.)

6. Confidentiality Obligation Survives Employment

This makes clear that the employee's duty not to disclose confidential information does not end when the job does. As long as the material remains a trade secret, the duty to keep it secret remains.

7. General Provisions

If you would like explanations of any of the following provisions, review Chapter 3:

- Relationships
- Severability
- Integration
- Waiver
- Injunctive Relief
- Indemnity
- Attorney Fees
- Governing Law
- Jurisdiction
- Successors & Assigns
- Signatures

B. Nondisclosure Agreement for Business Negotiations

Use this nondisclosure agreement when you're engaged in business negotiations—for example, merger or investment discussions, negotiations about joint ventures or talks with consultants or potential licensees.

 This Agreement may be found on the CD-ROM at the back of the book under the file name: BizNondisclose.rtf.

Nondisclosure Agreement for Business Negotiations

This agreement between _____ (the "Disclosing Party") and
_____ (the "Receiving Party") is effective _____.
It is entered into to prevent the unauthorized disclosure of Confidential Information (as
defined below) of Disclosing Party which may be disclosed to Receiving Party for the purpose
of pursuing or establishing a business relationship or negotiating a contract between the
parties. Accordingly, the parties agree as follows:

1. Confidential Information

[*Alternative 1*]
The following information constitutes confidential proprietary trade secret information
("Confidential Information") belonging to Disclosing Party: _____.

[*Alternative 2*]
Disclosing Party's confidential proprietary trade secret information ("Confidential
Information") consists of information and materials that are valuable and not generally known
by Disclosing Party's competitors. Confidential Information includes:

(a) Any and all information concerning Disclosing Party's current, future or proposed
products, including, but not limited to, formulas, designs, devices, computer code, drawings,
specifications, notebook entries, technical notes and graphs, computer printouts, technical
memoranda and correspondence, product development agreements and related agreements.

(b) Information and materials relating to Disclosing Party's purchasing, accounting and
marketing, including, but not limited to, marketing plans, sales data, business methods,
unpublished promotional material, cost and pricing information and customer lists.

(c) Information of the type described above which Disclosing Party obtained from another
party and which Disclosing Party treats as confidential, whether or not owned or developed
by Disclosing Party.

(d) Other: _____.

2. Nondisclosure

Receiving Party will treat Confidential Information with the same degree of care and
safeguards that it takes with its own Confidential Information, but in no event less than a
reasonable degree of care. Without Disclosing Party's prior written consent, Receiving Party
will not:

(a) disclose Confidential Information to any third party;

(b) make or permit to be made copies or other reproductions of Confidential Information; or

(c) make any commercial use of Confidential Information.

Receiving Party will carefully restrict access to Confidential Information to those of its officers, directors and employees who are subject to nondisclosure restrictions at least as protective as those set forth in this Agreement and who clearly need such access to participate on Receiving Party's behalf in the analysis and negotiation of a business relationship or any contract or agreement with Disclosing Party.

Receiving Party will advise each officer, director or employee to whom it provides access to any Confidential Information that they are prohibited from using it or disclosing it to others without Disclosing Party's prior written consent.

[*Optional*]
In addition, without prior written consent of Disclosing Party, Receiving Party shall not disclose to any person either the fact that discussions or negotiations are taking place concerning a possible transaction or the status of such discussions or negotiations.

3. Return of Materials

Upon Disclosing Party's request, Receiving Party shall within 30 days return all original materials provided by Disclosing Party and any copies, notes or other documents in Receiving Party's possession pertaining to Confidential Information.

4. Exclusions

This agreement does not apply to any information that:

(a) was in Receiving Party's possession or was known to Receiving Party, without an obligation to keep it confidential, before such information was disclosed to Receiving Party by Disclosing Party;

(b) is or becomes public knowledge through a source other than Receiving Party and through no fault of Receiving Party;

(c) is or becomes lawfully available to Receiving Party from a source other than Disclosing Party; or

(d) is disclosed by Receiving Party with Disclosing Party's prior written approval.

5. Term

[*Alternative 1*]
This Agreement and Receiving Party's duty to hold Confidential Information in confidence shall remain in effect until Confidential Information is no longer a trade secret or until Disclosing Party sends Receiving Party written notice releasing Receiving Party from this Agreement, whichever occurs first.

[*Alternative 2*]
This Agreement and Receiving Party's duty to hold Confidential Information in confidence shall remain in effect until _____ or until whichever of the following occurs first:

(a) Disclosing Party sends Receiving Party written notice releasing it from this Agreement, or

(b) Confidential Information disclosed under this Agreement ceases to be a trade secret.

6. No Rights Granted

This Agreement does not constitute a grant or an intention or commitment to grant any right, title or interest in Confidential Information to Receiving Party.

7. Warranty

Disclosing Party warrants that it has the right to make the disclosures under this Agreement.

8. General Provisions

(a) Relationships: Nothing contained in this Agreement shall be deemed to constitute either party a partner, joint venturer or employee of the other party for any purpose.

(b) Severability: If a court finds any provision of this Agreement invalid or unenforceable, the remainder of this Agreement shall be interpreted so as best to effect the intent of the parties.

(c) Integration: This Agreement expresses the complete understanding of the parties with respect to the subject matter and supersedes all prior proposals, agreements, representations and understandings. This Agreement may not be amended except in a writing signed by both parties.

(d) Waiver: The failure to exercise any right provided in this Agreement shall not be a waiver of prior or subsequent rights.

(e) Injunctive Relief: Any misappropriation of Confidential Information in violation of this Agreement may cause Disclosing Party irreparable harm, the amount of which may be difficult to ascertain, and therefore Receiving Party agrees that Disclosing Party shall have the right to apply to a court of competent jurisdiction for an order enjoining any such further misappropriation and for such other relief as Disclosing Party deems appropriate. This right of Disclosing Party is to be in addition to the remedies otherwise available to Disclosing Party.

(f) Indemnity: Receiving Party agrees to indemnify Disclosing Party against any and all losses, damages, claims or expenses incurred or suffered by Disclosing Party as a result of Receiving Party's breach of this Agreement.

(g) Attorney Fees and Expenses: In a dispute arising out of or related to this Agreement, the prevailing party shall have the right to collect from the other party its reasonable attorney fees and costs and necessary expenditures.

(h) Governing Law: This Agreement shall be governed in accordance with the laws of the State of _____.

(i) Jurisdiction: The parties consent to the exclusive jurisdiction and venue of the federal and state courts located in _____ [*insert county and state in which parties agree to litigate*] in any action arising out of or relating to this Agreement. The parties waive any other venue to which either party might be entitled by domicile or otherwise.

(j) Successors & Assigns:

[*Alternative 1*]
This Agreement shall bind each party's heirs, successors and assigns. Receiving Party may not assign or transfer its rights or obligations under this Agreement without the prior written consent of Disclosing Party. Any assignment or transfer in violation of this section shall be void.

[*Alternative 2 (Consent Not Unreasonably Withheld)*]
This Agreement shall bind each party's heirs, successors and assigns. Receiving Party may not assign or transfer its rights or obligations under this Agreement without the prior written consent of Disclosing Party. Such consent shall not be unreasonably withheld. Any assignment or transfer in violation of this section shall be void.

[Alternative 3 (Consent not needed for affiliates or new owners)]
This Agreement shall bind each party's heirs, successors and assigns. Receiving Party may not assign or transfer its rights or obligations under this Agreement without the prior written consent of Disclosing Party. However, no consent is required for an assignment or transfer that occurs: (a) to an entity in which Receiving Party owns more than fifty percent of the assets; or (b) as part of a transfer of all or substantially all of the assets of Receiving Party to any party. Any assignment or transfer in violation of this section shall be void.

Disclosing Party:

_____

(Signature)

_____

(Typed or Printed Name)

Title: _____

Date: _____

Receiving Party:

_____

(Signature)

_____

(Typed or Printed Name)

Title: _____

Date: _____

1. Introductory Paragraph

Fill in the date the agreement will take effect. This can be the date it's signed or a date in the future. Next, fill in your company name (you are the disclosing party). Finally, fill in the name of the outside individual or company being granted access to your trade secrets (the Receiving Party).

2. Confidential Information

Select either Alternative 1 or 2, and delete the other. Here's how to choose:

Alternative 1. Use this clause if you can individually list the material being provided. However, be careful that your description is not so narrowly worded that it may leave out important information you want covered by the agreement.

Alternative 2. Use this clause if it's not possible to specifically identify the trade secrets—for example, if the information to be disclosed does not yet exist. This clause contains a general description of the types of information covered.

3. Nondisclosure

This clause makes clear that your trade secrets must be kept in confidence by the receiving party and may not be revealed to others without your prior written consent. It contains an optional provision requiring the fact that negotiations taking place are to be kept secret.

4. Return of Materials

Here, the receiving party promises to return original materials provided by your company, as well as copies, notes and documents pertaining to the trade secrets. The form gives the receiving party 30 days to return the materials, but you can change this time period if you wish.

5. Exclusions

This provision describes all the types of information that are not covered by the agreement. These exclusions are based on court decisions and state trade secret laws that say these types of information do not qualify for trade secret protection.

6. Term

There are two alternate provisions dealing with how long the agreement will stay in effect. Select the clause that best suits your needs and delete the other:

Alternative 1. This provision has no definite time limit—in other words, the receiving party must keep mum until the trade secret ceases to be a trade secret. This may occur when the information becomes generally known, you disclose it to the public, or it ceases being a trade secret for some other reason. (See Chapter 1.) This gives you the broadest protection possible.

Alternative 2. Some receiving parties don't want to be subject to open-ended confidentiality obligations. Use this clause if the receiving party insists that the agreement contain a definite expiration date. The Agreement should last as long as the information is likely to remain a trade secret. Five years is a common period, but it can be much shorter, even as little as six months. In Internet and technology businesses, the time period may need to be shorter because of the fast pace of innovation.

7. No Rights Granted

This clause makes clear that you are not granting any ownership rights in the confidential information to the receiving party.

8. Warranty

A warranty is a promise. Here, you promise the receiving party that you have the right to disclose the information. This is intended to assure the receiving party that it won't be sued by some third party claiming that the trade secrets belonged to it and that you had no right to reveal them to the receiving party.

9. General Provisions

If you would like explanations for any of the following provisions, review Chapter 3:

- Relationships
- Severability
- Integration

- Waiver
- Injunctive Relief
- Indemnity
- Attorney Fees
- Governing Law
- Jurisdiction
- Assignments
- Successors
- Signatures

C. Visitor Nondisclosure Agreement

If visitors to your company might have access to company trade secrets, ask them to sign a nondisclosure agreement. We've removed many of the provisions from other NDAs in order to make this a short, easy-to-understand agreement; one that visitors shouldn't object to signing. Give visitors a signed copy.

 This Agreement may be found on the CD-ROM at the back of the book under the file name: VisitNondisclose.rtf.

Visitor Nondisclosure Agreement

Visitor's Name (*Print*): _____

Affiliation: _____

Place Visited: _____

Date(s) Visited: _____

1. I may be given access to confidential information belonging to
_____ (the "Company") through my relationship with Company or as
a result of my access to Company's premises.

2. I understand and acknowledge that Company's trade secrets consist of information and
materials that are valuable and not generally known by Company's competitors, including:

(a) Any and all information concerning Company's current, future or proposed products,
including, but not limited to, computer code, drawings, specifications, notebook entries,
technical notes and graphs, computer printouts, technical memoranda and correspondence,
product development agreements and related agreements.

(b) Information and materials relating to Company's purchasing, accounting and marketing;
including, but not limited to, marketing plans, sales data, unpublished promotional material,
cost and pricing information and customer lists.

(c) Information of the type described above which Company obtained from another party
and which Company treats as confidential, whether or not owned or developed by
Company.

(d) Other: _____.

3. In consideration of being admitted to Company's facilities, I will hold in the strictest
confidence any trade secrets or confidential information that is disclosed to me. I will not
remove any document, equipment or other materials from the premises without Company's
written permission. I will not photograph or otherwise record any information to which I may
have access during my visit.

4. This Agreement is binding on me, my heirs, executors, administrators and assigns and
inures to the benefit of Company, its successors and assigns.

5. This Agreement constitutes the entire understanding between Company and me with respect to its subject matter. It supersedes all earlier representations and understandings, whether oral or written.

Visitor:

_____

(Signature)

_____

(Typed or Printed Name)

Date: _____

1. Introductory Material

Visitor's Name: Fill in the name of the person who is visiting your company.

Affiliation:
Fill in the name of the company or organization the individual represents.

Place Visited:
Fill in your company's name and the address of the location visited.

Date Visited:
Fill in the date or dates of the visit.

2. Access to Confidential Information

Fill in your company's name.

3. Definition of Confidential Information

This clause defines what information the visitor must keep confidential. You have

the option of listing any specific items in section 2(d).

4. Obligation to Keep Trade Secrets Confidential

This clause spells out the visitor's confidentiality obligations. There's nothing to fill in here.

5. Successors

This clause makes the confidentiality obligations binding on the visitor even if the company is sold or goes out of business.

6. Entire Agreement

This clause makes clear that the agreement can't be changed except by a writing signed by the parties. There's nothing to fill in here.

7. Signature

Each visitor should sign and date the agreement, preferably before gaining access to trade secrets. (See Chapter 3, Section A7 for details on signatures.)

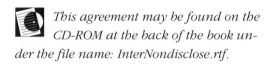

This agreement may be found on the CD-ROM at the back of the book under the file name: InterNondisclose.rtf.

D. Interview Nondisclosure Agreement

You may end up divulging trade secrets when interviewing prospective employees, especially for sensitive jobs. Any person you hire should be required to sign an employee NDA (or an employment agreement containing a nondisclosure provision). But, of course, the interviewees you don't hire won't be signing an employment NDA or employment agreement. For this reason, have applicants for sensitive positions sign a simple nondisclosure agreement at the beginning of a job interview.

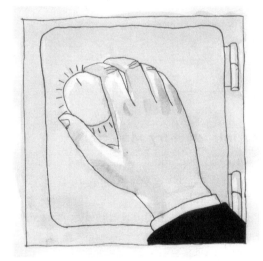

Interview Nondisclosure Agreement

_____ ("Company") and _____ ("Applicant") agree as follows:

1. Company is interviewing Applicant for the position of _____ and to work on the following projects: _____.

2. Company's trade secrets may be disclosed during the interview process or as a result of Applicant's access to Company's premises.

3. Company's trade secrets consist of information and materials that are valuable and not generally known by Company's competitors, including:

(a) Any and all information concerning Company's current, future or proposed products, including, but not limited to, computer code, drawings, specifications, notebook entries, technical notes and graphs, computer printouts, technical memoranda and correspondence, product development agreements and related agreements.

(b) Information and materials relating to Company's purchasing, accounting and marketing; including, but not limited to, marketing plans, sales data, unpublished promotional material, cost and pricing information and customer lists.

(c) Information of the type described above which Company obtained from another party and which Company treats as confidential, whether or not owned or developed by Company.

(d) Other: _____.

4. At all times, Applicant will keep confidential and will not make use of or disclose to any third party any of Company's trade secrets.

5. Applicant will not use, disclose to Company, or cause Company to use any trade secret or confidential information of any other person or entity.

Company:

_____
(Signature)

_____
(Typed or Printed Name)

Title: _____

Date: _____

Applicant:

_____
(Signature)

_____
(Typed or Printed Name)

Date: _____

1. Company Name

Fill in your company's name and the name of the job applicant.

2. Job

Describe the position or projects the applicant is being interviewed for.

3. Possible Disclosure of Confidential Information

This just states that the applicant might learn trade secrets during the interviewing process. There is nothing to fill in.

4. Definition of Confidential Information

This describes the kinds of material the applicant might see that you consider trade secrets. Fill in Section 3(d) if the information to be disclosed is not listed elsewhere in this section.

5. Obligation to Keep Trade Secrets Confidential

This informs the applicant that he or she cannot disclose the information.

6. Other Companies' Trade Secrets

Here, the applicant promises not to reveal confidential information from any other company during the interview or at another time.

7. Signatures

See Chapter 3, Section A7 for details on signatures.

E. Software Beta Tester Nondisclosure Agreement

If you develop software (including Web applications) and give beta versions to outside testers, here is a nondisclosure agreement for you to use.

 This agreement may be found on the CD-ROM at the back of the book under the file name: BetaNondisclosure.rtf.

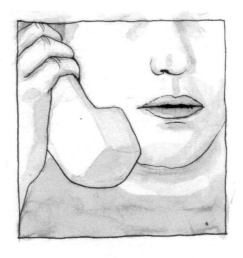

Software Beta Tester Nondisclosure Agreement

This is an agreement, effective _____, between _____ ("Company") and _____ ("Tester"), in which Tester agrees to test a software program known as _____ (the "Software") and keep Company aware of the test results.

1. Company's Obligations

Company shall provide Tester with a copy of Software and any necessary documentation and instruct Tester on how to use it and what test data is desired by Company. Upon satisfactory completion of the testing,

[*Choose one*]

❏ Company shall furnish Tester with one free copy of the production version of Software, contingent upon Company's decision to proceed with production of Software.

❏ _____.

Tester shall be entitled to the same benefits to which regular purchasers of Software will be entitled.

2. Tester's Obligations

Tester shall test Software under normally expected operating conditions in Tester's environment during the test period. Tester shall gather and report test data as agreed upon with Company. Tester shall allow Company access to Software during normal working hours for inspection, modifications and maintenance.

3. Software a Trade Secret

Software is proprietary to, and a valuable trade secret of, Company. It is entrusted to Tester only for the purpose set forth in this Agreement. Tester shall maintain Software in the strictest confidence. Tester will not, without Company's prior written consent:

(a) disclose any information about Software, its design and performance specifications, its code, and the existence of the beta test and its results to anyone other than Tester's employees who are performing the testing and who shall be subject to nondisclosure restrictions at least as protective as those set forth in this Agreement;

(b) copy any portion of Software or documentation, except to the extent necessary to perform beta testing; or

(c) reverse engineer, decompile or disassemble Software or any portion of it.

4. Security Precautions

Tester shall take reasonable security precautions to prevent Software from being seen by unauthorized individuals whether stored on Tester's hard drive or on physical copies such as CD-ROMS, diskettes or other media. Tester shall lock all copies of Software and associated documentation in a desk or file cabinet when not in use.

5. Term of Agreement

The test period shall last from _____, until _____. This Agreement shall terminate at the end of the test period or when Company asks Tester to return Software, whichever occurs first. The restrictions and obligations contained in Clauses 4, 7, 8, 9 and 10 shall survive the expiration, termination or cancellation of this Agreement, and shall continue to bind Tester, its successors, heirs and assigns.

6. Return of Software and Materials

Upon the conclusion of the testing period or at Company's request, Tester shall within 10 days return the original and all copies of Software and all related materials to Company and delete all portions of Software from computer memory.

7. Disclaimer of Warranty

Software is a test product and its accuracy and reliability are not guaranteed. Tester shall not rely exclusively on Software for any reason. Tester waives any and all claims Tester may have against Company arising out of the performance or nonperformance of Software.

SOFTWARE IS PROVIDED AS IS, AND COMPANY DISCLAIMS ANY AND ALL REPRESENTATIONS OR WARRANTIES OF ANY KIND, WHETHER EXPRESS OR IMPLIED, WITH RESPECT TO IT, INCLUDING ANY IMPLIED WARRANTIES OF MERCHANTABILITY OR FITNESS FOR A PARTICULAR PURPOSE.

8. Limitation of Liability

Company shall not be responsible for any loss or damage to Tester or any third parties caused by Software. COMPANY SHALL NOT BE LIABLE FOR ANY DIRECT, INDIRECT, SPECIAL, INCIDENTAL OR CONSEQUENTIAL DAMAGE, WHETHER BASED ON CONTRACT OR TORT OR ANY OTHER LEGAL THEORY, ARISING OUT OF ANY USE OF SOFTWARE OR ANY PERFORMANCE OF THIS AGREEMENT.

9. No Rights Granted

This Agreement does not constitute a grant or an intention or commitment to grant any right, title or interest in Software or Company's trade secrets to Tester. Tester may not sell or transfer any portion of Software to any third party or use Software in any manner to produce, market or support its own products. Tester shall not identify Software as coming from any source other than Company.

10. No Assignments

This Agreement is personal to Tester. Tester shall not assign or otherwise transfer any rights or obligations under this Agreement.

11. General Provisions

(a) Relationships: Nothing contained in this Agreement shall be deemed to constitute either party a partner, joint venturer or employee of the other party for any purpose.

(b) Severability: If a court finds any provision of this Agreement invalid or unenforceable, the remainder of this Agreement shall be interpreted so as best to effect the intent of the parties.

(c) Integration: This Agreement expresses the complete understanding of the parties with respect to the subject matter and supersedes all prior proposals, agreements, representations and understandings. This Agreement may not be amended except in a writing signed by both parties.

(d) Waiver: The failure to exercise any right provided in this Agreement shall not be a waiver of prior or subsequent rights.

(e) Attorney Fees and Expenses: In a dispute arising out of or related to this Agreement, the prevailing party shall have the right to collect from the other party its reasonable attorney fees and costs and necessary expenditures.

(f) Governing Law: This Agreement shall be governed in accordance with the laws of the State of _____.

(g) Jurisdiction: The parties consent to the exclusive jurisdiction and venue of the federal and state courts located in _____ [insert county and state in which parties agree to litigate] in any action arising out of or relating to this Agreement. The parties waive any other venue to which either party might be entitled by domicile or otherwise.

Company:

_____

(Signature)

_____

(Typed or Printed Name)

Title: _____

Date: _____

Tester:

_____

(Signature)

_____

(Typed or Printed Name)

Date: _____

1. Introductory Paragraph

Fill in the date. Next, fill in your name. Fill in the name of the outside individual or company that is beta-testing your software (the "Tester").

2. Software

Here, fill in the name of the software being tested.

3. Company's Obligations

Typically, a beta tester is given a free copy of the finished version of software as payment. That is what this agreement provides, although you can make some other arrangements for payment—for example, an hourly rate or a fixed fee.

4. Tester's Obligations

This clause describes the software tester's duties, which are to gather and report test data. There is nothing to add here.

5. Software a Trade Secret

This clause makes clear to the tester that the software is a trade secret. The tester is not allowed to copy the software except as necessary to perform or test it and may not reverse engineer or disassemble it to see how it works.

6. Security Precautions

This clause requires the tester to take reasonable precautions to make sure the software isn't seen by unauthorized people. There is nothing to add here.

7. Term of Agreement

Fill in the time frame during which the testing will occur.

8. Return of Software and Materials

This clause requires the tester to return the software when the testing is done and delete it from any computer on which it's been installed.

9. Disclaimer of Warranty

This clause states that the software is being provided to the tester "as is." You do not guarantee the software for any purpose and the tester waives any potential legal claims against your company arising from the use of the software—for example, if it does not perform the claimed functions.

10. Limitation of Liability

This clause makes it clear to the beta tester that the software is being provided only for evaluation purposes, and that you are not liable for any damages caused by the beta tester's use of the software—for example, if it damages the tester's hard drive.

11. No Rights Granted

This clause makes it absolutely clear that the software belongs to you and that the tester is acquiring no ownership rights in it whatsoever and cannot sell or transfer the software to others.

12. No Assignments

This clause provides that the tester must perform the testing services personally. The tester may not get anyone else to do the testing.

13. General Provisions

If you would like explanations of any of the following provisions, review Chapter 3:

- Relationships
- Severability
- Integration
- Waiver
- Attorney Fees
- Governing Law
- Jurisdiction
- Signatures

This agreement may be found on the CD-ROM at the back of the book under the file name: Nondisclosure.rtf.

F. Prospective Licensee Nondisclosure Agreement for Software Company

If your company produces software, you'll need a nondisclosure agreement when you provide a copy of a finished software product to a prospective licensee or other customer for evaluation.

Nondisclosure Agreement for Licensee

This agreement, effective _____ between _____ ("Company")
and _____ ("Customer"), is entered into to authorize Customer to
receive from Company and evaluate certain proprietary computer software and
documentation known as _____, ("Software").

1. Nonexclusive License

Company grants Customer a nonexclusive license to install Software on its computer system
and use Software for a period of _____ days from the date of delivery. Customer shall
use Software only for the purpose of evaluating its performance and not for a productive
purpose. Customer shall acquire no other intellectual property rights under this Agreement.

2. Software a Trade Secret

Software is proprietary to, and a valuable trade secret of, Company.

3. Nondisclosure

In consideration of Company's disclosure of Software to Customer, Customer will treat
Software with the same degree of care and safeguards that it takes with its own trade
secrets, but in no event less than a reasonable degree of care. Customer will not, without
Company's prior written consent:

(a) reverse engineer, decompile or disassemble Software or any portion of it;

(b) copy any portion of Software;

(c) download Software in a retrieval system or computer system of any kind except as
authorized by this Agreement; or

(d) disclose any portion of Software to any third party.

Customer will limit use of Software to those employees, agents and consultants of Customer
who are performing the evaluation for Customer. Customer must advise such people that
Software is Company's trade secret and they must be under an express written obligation to
maintain its confidentiality.

The restrictions and obligations contained in this clause will remain in effect until Software no
longer constitutes a trade secret or until Company sends Customer written notice releasing it
from this Agreement, whichever occurs first.

4. Return of Software and Materials

Customer shall promptly return Software and all related materials to Company and delete all copies and portions of Software from computer memory upon the termination of this Agreement, Company's request, or the Customer's decision not to purchase or license Software, whichever occurs first.

5. Limitation of Liability

Company shall not be responsible for any loss or damage to Customer or any third parties caused by Customer's use of Software.

COMPANY SHALL NOT BE LIABLE FOR ANY DIRECT, INDIRECT, SPECIAL, INCIDENTAL OR CONSEQUENTIAL DAMAGES, WHETHER BASED ON CONTRACT OR TORT OR ANY OTHER LEGAL THEORY, ARISING OUT OF ANY USE OF SOFTWARE OR ANY PERFORMANCE OF THIS AGREEMENT.

6. General Provisions

(a) Relationships: Nothing contained in this Agreement shall be deemed to constitute either party a partner, joint venturer or employee of the other party for any purpose.

(b) Severability: If a court finds any provision of this Agreement invalid or unenforceable, the remainder of this Agreement shall be interpreted so as best to effect the intent of the parties.

(c) Integration: This Agreement expresses the complete understanding of the parties with respect to the subject matter and supersedes all prior proposals, agreements, representations and understandings. This Agreement may not be amended except in a writing signed by both parties.

(d) Waiver: The failure to exercise any right provided in this Agreement shall not be a waiver of prior or subsequent rights.

(e) Injunctive Relief: Customer acknowledges that any misappropriation of any of the Confidential Information in violation of this Agreement may cause Company irreparable harm, the amount of which may be difficult to ascertain, and therefore agrees that Company shall have the right to apply to a court of competent jurisdiction for an order enjoining any such further misappropriation and for such other relief as Company deems appropriate. This right of Company is to be in addition to the remedies otherwise available to Company.

(f) Indemnity: Customer agrees to indemnify Company against any and all losses, damages, claims or expenses incurred or suffered by Company as a result of the Customer's breach of this Agreement.

(g) Attorney Fees and Expenses: In a dispute arising out of or related to this Agreement, the prevailing party shall have the right to collect from the other party its reasonable attorney fees and costs and necessary expenditures.

(h) Governing Law: This Agreement shall be governed in accordance with the laws of the State of _____.

(i) Jurisdiction: The parties consent to the exclusive jurisdiction and venue of the federal and state courts located in_____ [*insert county and state in which parties agree to litigate*] in any action arising out of or relating to this Agreement. The parties waive any other venue to which either party might be entitled by domicile or otherwise.

(j) Successors and Assigns: This Agreement shall bind each party's heirs, successors and assigns. Customer may not assign or transfer its rights or obligations under this Agreement without the prior written consent of Company. Any assignment or transfer in violation of this section shall be void.

Company:

_____

(Signature)

_____

(Typed or Printed Name)

Title: _____

Date: _____

Customer:

_____

(Signature)

_____

(Typed or Printed Name)

Date: _____

1. Introductory Paragraph

Fill in the date you want the agreement to take effect. Next, fill in your company name. Fill in the name of the outside individual or company being granted access to your trade secrets (called the "Customer"). Finally, describe the software or other information disclosed or fill in the name of the product.

2. Nonexclusive License

Fill in the number of days you are allowing the customer to use the software for evaluation purposes.

3. Software a Trade Secret

This clause makes it clear that the software is a trade secret. There is nothing to fill in here.

4. Nondisclosure

This provision is the heart of the agreement. The customer promises to treat your trade secrets with a reasonable degree of care and not to disclose them to third parties without your written consent. The customer also promises not to make commercial use of the information without your permission.

Finally, the customer may not disclose the information to its employees or consultants unless they have signed confidentiality agreements protecting your trade secrets. If the customer breaks these promises, you can sue to obtain monetary dam-ages and possibly a court order to prevent the customer from using the information.

5. Return of Software and Materials

This clause outlines when the product must be returned to your company.

6. Limitation of Liability

This clause makes it clear to the customer that the software is being provided only for evaluation purposes and that you are not liable for any damages caused by the customer's use of the software.

7. General Provisions

If you would like explanations of any of the following provisions, review Chapter 3:

- Relationships
- Severability
- Integration
- Waiver
- Injunctive Relief
- Indemnity
- Attorney Fees
- Governing Law
- Jurisdiction
- Assignments
- Successors
- Signatures

G. Student Nondisclosure Agreement

Universities, colleges, research labs and similar institutions often engage the services of students as researchers or assistants and want to make sure they don't reveal trade secrets without permission. This agreement accomplishes just that. For-profit businesses that hire students under work/study programs or as regular employees should use the employee form in Section A.

 This agreement may be found on the CD-ROM at the back of the book under the file name: StudNondisclose.rtf.

Student Nondisclosure Agreement

In consideration of being given access to information that will be valuable for my research or study in the area of: _____[*describe*] by _____
[*full name of university or college*] ("Disclosing Party"), I agree as follows:

1. Trade Secrets

I understand that during the course of my study and/or research there may be disclosed to me or I may gain access to trade secrets and other proprietary or confidential information of Disclosing Party. This includes, but is not limited to:

(a) technical information concerning Disclosing Party's research projects, technical memoranda and correspondence, formulas, designs, devices, diagrams, software code, test results, processes, inventions; and

(b) Disclosing Party's business information, including cost information, accounting and unpublished financial information, business plans, customer lists and customer information, purchasing techniques, supplier lists and supplier information and marketing, production or merchandising systems or plans;

2. Nondisclosure of Trade Secrets

I will keep Disclosing Party's trade secrets, whether or not prepared or developed by me, in the strictest confidence. I will not disclose such secrets to anyone outside Disclosing Party without Disclosing Party's prior written consent. Nor will I make use of any Disclosing Party trade secrets for my own purposes or the benefit of anyone other than Disclosing Party without Disclosing Party's prior written consent.

However, I have no obligation to treat as confidential any information which:

(a) was in my possession or known to me, without an obligation to keep it confidential, before such information was disclosed to me by Disclosing Party;

(b) is or becomes public knowledge through a source other than me and through no fault of Employee; or

(c) is or becomes lawfully available to me from a source other than Disclosing Party.

3. Return of Materials

When my research or study with Disclosing Party ends, for whatever reason, I will promptly deliver to Disclosing Party all originals and copies of all documents, records, software programs, media and other materials containing any of Disclosing Party's trade secrets. I will also return to Disclosing Party all equipment, files, software programs and other personal property belonging to Disclosing Party.

4. Review of Papers or Publications

For a period of _____ years, I will submit to _____ [Name] a full and complete draft of any papers, reports or proposed publications that include any information derived from my research or study with Disclosing Party for its review. I shall disguise or excise from this material any data that Disclosing Party identifies as too sensitive for disclosure.

5. Duration of Confidentiality Obligation

My obligation to maintain the confidentiality and security of Disclosing Party's trade secrets continues for so long as such material remains a trade secret.

6. General Provisions

(a) Relationships: Nothing contained in this Agreement shall be deemed to make me a partner, joint venturer or employee of Disclosing Party for any purpose.

(b) Severability: If a court finds any provision of this Agreement invalid or unenforceable, the remainder of this Agreement shall be interpreted so as best to effect the intent of Disclosing Party and myself.

(c) Integration: This Agreement expresses the complete understanding of the parties with respect to the subject matter and supersedes all prior proposals, agreements, representations and understandings. This Agreement may not be amended except in a writing signed by both Disclosing Party and myself.

(d) Waiver: The failure to exercise any right provided in this Agreement shall not be a waiver of prior or subsequent rights.

(e) Injunctive Relief: I acknowledge that any misappropriation of any of the Confidential Information in violation of this Agreement may cause Disclosing Party irreparable harm, the amount of which may be difficult to ascertain, and therefore agree that Disclosing Party shall have the right to apply to a court of competent jurisdiction for an order enjoining any such further misappropriation and for such other relief as Disclosing Party deems appropriate. This right is to be in addition to the remedies otherwise available to Disclosing Party.

(f) Indemnity: I agree to indemnify Disclosing Party against any and all losses, damages, claims or expenses incurred or suffered by Disclosing Party as a result of my breach of this Agreement.

(g) Attorney Fees and Expenses: In a dispute arising out of or related to this Agreement, the prevailing party shall have the right to collect from the other party its reasonable attorney fees and costs and necessary expenditures.

(h) Governing Law. This Agreement shall be governed in accordance with the laws of the State of _____.

(i) Jurisdiction. I consent to the exclusive jurisdiction and venue of the federal and state courts located in_____ [*insert county and state in which parties agree to litigate*] in any action arising out of or relating to this Agreement. I waive any other venue to which I might be entitled by domicile or otherwise.

(j) Successors & Assigns. This Agreement shall bind each party's heirs, successors and assigns. Disclosing Party may assign this Agreement to any party at any time. I shall not assign any of its rights or obligations under this Agreement without Disclosing Party's prior written consent. Any assignment or transfer in violation of this section shall be void.

7. Signature

I have carefully read and considered all clauses of this Agreement and agree that all of the restrictions set forth are fair and reasonably required to protect Disclosing Party's interests. I have received a copy of this Agreement as signed by me.

Student:

_____

(Signature)

_____

(Typed or Printed Name)

Date: _____

1. Introductory Paragraph

In the first paragraph describe briefly the general area of study or research the student will be involved in. Then provide the full name of the college, university or other institution. For the sake of convenience, this entity is called the "disclosing party" in the rest of the agreement.

2. Trade Secrets

This paragraph describes in general terms the types of information the student may not disclose without prior permission. This includes both technical information and business information. There is nothing to add here.

3. Nondisclosure of Trade Secrets

This paragraph requires the student to keep the disclosing party's trade secrets confidential. This clause explains, however, that the student's nondisclosure obligation does not extend to:

- information the student knew before studying with disclosing party
- information learned from sources outside the disclosing party, or
- information that is public knowledge (so long as the employee didn't make it public).

4. Return of Materials

This paragraph requires the student to return all trade secret materials to the disclosing party when the term of research or study ends. There is nothing to add here.

5. Review of Papers or Publications

This paragraph requires the student to submit to a named individual any papers or proposed publications. This way you can make sure they don't contain any trade secrets you don't want published or otherwise disclosed to the public.

6. Duration of Confidentiality Obligation

This paragraph provides that the student's obligation to maintain the confidentiality of the trade secrets lasts as long as the information remains a trade secret.

7. General Provisions

If you would like explanations of any of the following provisions, review Chapter 3:

- Relationships
- Severability
- Integration
- Waiver
- Injunctive Relief
- Indemnity
- Attorney Fees
- Governing Law
- Jurisdiction
- Assignments
- Successors & Assigns
- Signatures

H. Customer List/Mailing List Nondisclosure Agreement

Many companies sell or license their customer lists to other businesses. For example, a magazine publisher may sell its subscriber lists to an advertiser who wants to target readers by direct mail. You can use this NDA whenever your company provides a customer list or mailing list to another company. Here's how to fill it out.

 This agreement may be found on the CD-ROM at the back of the book under the file name:ListNondisclose.rtf.

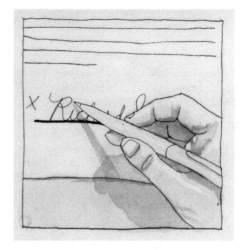

Customer List/Mailing List Nondisclosure Agreement

For valuable consideration, the receipt and sufficiency of which is hereby acknowledged, _____[*Full name of company*] ("Disclosing Party") authorizes _____[*Full name of receiving party*] ("Receiving Party") to use the customer list/mailing list identified as _____ [*Provide name for list*] ("List") under the following terms and conditions:

1. List a Trade Secret

Receiving Party understands and acknowledges that List is a valuable trade secret belonging to Disclosing Party.

2. Purpose of Disclosure

Receiving Party shall use the List only for the following purposes: _____ [*Describe—for example "to distribute Receiving Party's advertising or promotional material."*]

3. Receiving Party's Obligations

Receiving Party shall hold and maintain the List in the strictest confidence. Receiving Party shall carefully restrict access to the List only to persons bound by this Agreement and only on a need-to-know basis. Receiving Party shall not, without Disclosing Party's prior written approval, publish, copy, or otherwise disclose the List to others, or permit its use by others for their benefit or to Disclosing Party's detriment.

4. Term

[*Alternative 1*]
This Agreement and Receiving Party's duty to hold the List in confidence shall remain in effect until the List is no longer a trade secret or until Disclosing Party sends Receiving Party written notice releasing Receiving Party from this Agreement, whichever occurs first.

[*Alternative 2*]
This Agreement and Receiving Party's duty to hold the List in confidence shall remain in effect until _____ or until whichever of the following occurs first:

(a) Disclosing Party sends Receiving Party written notice releasing Receiving Party from this Agreement, or

(b) The List is no longer a trade secret.

5. No Rights Granted

Receiving Party understands and agrees that this Agreement does not constitute a grant or an intention or commitment to grant any right, title or interest in the List or any other of Disclosing Party's trade secrets to Receiving Party.

6. Warranty

Disclosing Party warrants that it has the right to make the disclosures under this Agreement.

7. General Provisions

(a) Relationships: Nothing contained in this Agreement shall be deemed to constitute either party a partner, joint venturer or employee of the other party for any purpose.

(b) Severability: If a court finds any provision of this Agreement invalid or unenforceable, the remainder of this Agreement shall be interpreted so as best to effect the intent of the parties.

(c) Integration: This Agreement expresses the complete understanding of the parties with respect to the subject matter and supersedes all prior proposals, agreements, representations and understandings. This Agreement may not be amended except in a writing signed by both parties.

(d) Waiver: The failure to exercise any right provided in this Agreement shall not be a waiver of prior or subsequent rights.

(e) Injunctive Relief: Receiving Party acknowledges that any misappropriation of any of the Confidential Information in violation of this Agreement may cause Disclosing Party irreparable harm, the amount of which may be difficult to ascertain, and therefore agrees that Disclosing Party shall have the right to apply to a court of competent jurisdiction for an order enjoining any such further misappropriation and for such other relief as Disclosing Party deems appropriate. This right of Disclosing Party is to be in addition to the remedies otherwise available to Disclosing Party.

(f) Indemnity: Receiving Party agrees to indemnify Disclosing Party against any and all losses, damages, claims or expenses incurred or suffered by Disclosing Party as a result of Receiving Party's breach of this Agreement.

(g) Attorney Fees and Expenses: In a dispute arising out of or related to this Agreement, the prevailing party shall have the right to collect from the other party its reasonable attorney fees and costs and necessary expenditures.

(h) Governing Law: This Agreement shall be governed in accordance with the laws of the State of _____.

(i) Jurisdiction: The parties consent to the exclusive jurisdiction and venue of the federal and state courts located in _____[*insert county and state in which parties agree to litigate*] in any action arising out of or relating to this Agreement. The parties waive any other venue to which either party might be entitled by domicile or otherwise.

(j) Successors & Assigns: This Agreement shall bind each party's heirs, successors and assigns. Receiving Party may not assign or transfer its rights or obligations under this Agreement without the prior written consent of Disclosing Party. Any assignment or transfer in violation of this section shall be void.

Disclosing Party:

_____

(Signature)

_____

(Typed or Printed Name)

Title: _____

Date: _____

Receiving Party:

_____

(Signature)

_____

(Typed or Printed Name)

Title: _____

Date: _____

1. Introduction

Where indicated, list the full names of the company or person providing the list (called the "Company" in the remainder of the agreement), and the company or person receiving the list (called the "Receiving Party"). Also identify the list, either by name or some other way.

2. List a Trade Secret

This clause makes clear that the list is your trade secret.

3. Purpose of Disclosure

State here how the receiving party will be allowed to use the list—for example, for advertising purposes. The receiving party will need to get your permission for any uses not listed here.

4. Receiving Party's Obligations

This clause requires the receiving party to treat the list as a trade secret. The receiving party may not disclose the list to others without your permission.

5. Term

This clause states how long the receiving party's confidentiality obligations will last. You'll need to pick one of two alternatives. The first alternative provides the longest term possible—the receiving party must keep the list confidential until it is no longer a trade secret or you release the

receiving party from the confidentiality obligation. This provision favors you.

The second alternative specifies an end date. Usually this is anywhere from six months to five years.

6. No Rights Granted

This clause is intended to make clear that the receiving party is not acquiring any ownership rights in the list by virtue of this agreement.

7. Warranty

A warranty is a promise. In this provision, you promise the receiving party that you have the right to disclose the list. This is intended to assure the receiving party that it won't be sued by some third party claiming that the list belonged to it and that you had no right to reveal it to the receiving party.

8. General Provisions

If you would like explanations of any of the following provisions, review Chapter 3:

- Relationships
- Severability
- Integration
- Waiver
- Injunctive Relief
- Indemnity
- Attorney Fees
- Governing Law
- Jurisdiction
- Successors & Assigns
- Signatures ∎

5

Who Owns a Trade Secret?

You can't enforce an NDA unless the secrets you're trying to protect really belong to you. But if an employee or independent contractor working for your company creates a trade secret, do you really own it?

This chapter explains the rules for trade secrets created by employees or independent contractors, and how to make sure your employees know that any trade secret they develop belongs to you and is covered by an NDA.

It's not possible to discuss ownership of trade secrets without discussing ownership of patents and copyrights. That's because trade secrets can also be the subject of patent or copyright protection. (See Chapter 1.) So, we also discuss rules that determine who owns these forms of intellectual property.

A. Trade Secrets Created by Employees

The most prudent means of guaranteeing your company's ownership of a trade secret developed by your employees is to use a written agreement. (It's possible, under certain circumstances, for an employer to acquire rights to an employee-created trade secret without a written agreement under legal rules known as "employed to invent" and "work made for hire," discussed in Section B.)

Two types of agreements work: an agreement signed before the employee begins working for you, or one signed after work has started, called an assignment. An agreement signed during or after employment requires additional payment.

California Law Establishes Trade Secret Ownership

California is unique in that its laws expressly establish that the employer owns trade secrets created by an employee. (Cal. Labor Code § 2860). However, an employer in California would not own trade secrets created on an employee's own time without the use of employee materials. (See Section A2e.) Although the law does not require a contract, it's a good idea to buttress your position in California by the use of a written agreement.

1. Agreements with Employees

Most employers don't use written employment agreements, which are a traditional place to put language giving the company ownership of employee creations. If you don't use employment agreements, your ownership of employee-created trade secrets can be established in the employee's NDA. The terms of ownership are in the Sample Employer Ownership Provisions, below, and can be added to the employee NDA in Chapter 4.

This language states that you own any intellectual property created by your employee. If the employee disregards the agreement and attempts to disclose, use, sell or license a trade secret created after signing the agreement, you will be able to sue for breach of the NDA, among other things. You could also sue for violation of state trade secret laws (see Appendix A) and if the trade secret is also subject to patent or copyright protection, for infringement.

2. Terms of the Agreement

Sample language you can include in an employee NDA or employment agreement appears below. An explanation of each provision follows the sample language.

 These provisions may be found on the CD-ROM forms disk at the back of the book under the file name: EmplOwnProvisions.rtf.

Sample Employer Ownership Provisions

Assignment of Intellectual Property. Employee agrees that any trade secret, process, system, discovery, improvement, copyrightable work of authorship or patentable creation (Innovations) conceived, originated, discovered or developed in whole or in part by Employee: (1) as a result of any work performed by Employee with Company's equipment, supplies, facilities, trade secret information, or other Company resources; or (2) on Company's time shall be the sole and exclusive property of Company, provided that the Innovation relates to Company's business or anticipated research. Employee acknowledges that any copyrightable works created within the course of employment are works made for hire as defined under copyright law. Employee agrees to sign and deliver to Company (either during or subsequent to Employee's employment) such documents as Company considers desirable to evidence Employee's assignment of rights or Company's ownership of such Innovations. All documentation or records reflecting any Innovations belong exclusively to Company and shall be delivered to Company by Employee when Employee is no longer employed by Company.

Power of Attorney. In the event Company is unable to secure Employee's signature on any document necessary to apply for, prosecute, obtain or enforce any legal right or protection relating to any Innovation or copyrightable work referred to above, Employee irrevocably designates and appoints Company (and each of its duly authorized officers and agents) as Employee's agent and attorney-in-fact, to act for and in Employee's behalf and to execute and file any such document and to do all other lawfully permitted acts to further the prosecution, issuance and enforcement of patents, copyrights or other rights.

Duty to Disclose. Employee agrees to promptly disclose in writing to Company all discoveries, developments, designs, code, ideas, innovations, improvements, trade secrets, formulas, processes, techniques, know-how, and data (whether or not patentable or registrable under copyright or similar statutes) made, written, conceived, reduced to practice or learned by Employee (either alone or jointly with others) that are related to or useful in Company's business, or that result from tasks assigned to Employee by Company, or from the use of facilities owned, leased or otherwise acquired by Company.

a. Assignment of Intellectual Property

This essential section guarantees you ownership of trade secrets, patents or copyrights created by your employee. You are claiming ownership only of work performed with company resources or on company time. Some employers go further and demand ownership of all innovations created during the employment period. We do not recommend this approach. If it were challenged in a court, a judge might consider it too broad or in violation of state laws (see, "Limitations on Employment Agreements," below), and declare the agreement invalid.

b. Power of Attorney

This provision allows you to exercise ownership rights without the employee and, if required for copyright, patent or other forms of protection, to register them with the government.

c. Duty to Disclose

This provision requires that the employee report any new discoveries to the company. This applies to any trade secrets or other innovations made by the employee that relate to your business, result from tasks assigned by the company, or are created using the company's resources. The purpose of the provision is to allow you to evaluate these employee-created properties and determine if the company has any rights. If intellectual property is created with an employee's own resources and is outside the scope of your business, the employee will not need to disclose it.

> **EXAMPLE 1:** Jessica works at an Internet search engine company and has signed an agreement requiring disclosure of all innovations that relate to her employment. At home, she conceives of a new method to sort search engine results. She must disclose the innovation to her employer.

> **EXAMPLE 2:** At home, Jessica also comes up with a device for measuring blood pressure in lab animals. She is not obligated to disclose the innovation to her employer.

d. Prior Inventions

Many employers also require that an employee disclose (and include as an exhibit to the agreement) any inventions, improvements or developments created by or owned by the employee. These inventions are then excluded from employer ownership under the agreement. You probably will not need to include this for most employees. However, if you are hiring a scientist, engineer or tech person with a history of creative developments, you may want to document who owns what. To include this, add the following language at the end of the "Duty to Disclose" section and attach a list (labeled "Exhibit A") of the employee's innovations.

Employee has created, co-created or claims an ownership interest in the inventions, discoveries or trade secrets (whether or not patentable or registrable under copyright or similar statutes) listed in Exhibit A, attached to this agreement and incorporated by reference.

---

e. State Law Limitations on These Agreements

Seven states (California, Delaware, Illinois, Kansas, Minnesota, North Carolina, and Washington) have laws that prohibit companies from attempting to acquire ownership of all employee inventions, regardless of where or how they are created. These laws prevent you from claiming ownership of an innovation or confidential information as part of an agreement if the material:

- is created with the employee's resources
- does not result from work performed for you, and
- does not relate to your business.

The Sample Employer Ownership Provisions, above, do not conflict with these laws. If you operate in one of these seven states and require an employer to sign an agreement violating the law, the agreement would be invalid.

Pre-Invention Assignment Statutes	
California	Cal. Lab. Code §§ 2870-72
Delaware	Del. Code Ann. tit. 19 § 805
Illinois	765 Ill. Comp. Stat § 1060/2
Kansas	Kan. Stat. Ann. §44-1306
Minnesota	Minn. Stat. § 181.78
North Carolina	N.C. Gen. Stat. §§ 66-57.1-.2
Washington	Wash. Rev. Code Ann. §§ 49.44.140, .150

The California statute also requires an employer to inform employees about the law. Adding a statement to the employment agreement usually does this:

> Innovations that qualify fully under the provisions of California Labor Code § 2870 and following shall not be subject to this provision.

B. If You Don't Have a Written Ownership Agreement With Your Employee

Even without a written agreement, state and federal laws guarantee you ownership of most trade secrets created by your employees in the course of employment. As a result, your NDA covering those secrets should be valid and enforceable. And even if you do not own an employee-created trade secret innovation, you may still have a nonexclusive right to use it.

1. Trade Secrets

If you hire someone to create a trade secret—for example, a process, formula, software program, method of doing business or mechanical invention—then the secrets the employee comes up with belong to the company even if you don't have an agreement that says so specifically. The rule is called the "employed to invent" doctrine, which was established by the U.S. Supreme Court more than a century ago. The court ruled, "That which [an employee] has been employed and paid to accomplish becomes, when accomplished, the property of his employer. Whatever rights as an individual he may have had in and to his inventive powers, and that which they are able to accomplish, he has sold in advance to his employer." *Solomons v. United States*, 137 U.S. 342 (1890).

How does this rule apply? If you hire someone because of his or her inventing or designing skills, or to create a specific innovation, you would own all rights to the employee's subsequent creation.

> **EXAMPLE:** An engineer had no written employment agreement with his employer. He was assigned as the chief engineer on a project to devise a method of welding a "leading edge" for turbine engines. The engineer spent at least 70% of his time on the project. He developed a hot forming process (HFP) for welding a leading edge and perfected the process on his employer's time and using his employer's employees, tools and materials. The engineer claimed that he was the sole owner.
>
> A court held that the company owned the rights to the HFP process because the engineer was hired for the express purpose of creating it. That fact, combined with the use of

the employer's supplies, payment for the work and the payment by the employer for the patent registration, demonstrated that there was an implied contract to assign the rights to the employer. *Teets v. Chromalloy Gas Turbine Corp.*, 83 F.3d 403 (CAFC 1996).

Despite this rule, we recommend that you always use a written agreement that clarifies ownership of all trade secrets. Signed agreements are more reliable and easier to enforce than an implied agreement and they ensure that your employees don't mistakenly believe they own trade secrets developed while working for you.

2. Shop Rights

An employer who does not own a trade secret under a written agreement or under "employed to invent" principles may still acquire a limited right to use the trade secret. This is called a shop right. The employee owns the trade secret, and is not bound to secrecy by the NDA, but the employer has a right to use the information without paying the creator. The shop right principle is derived from state laws and court cases and applies to both employees and independent contractors. A shop right can arise only if the employee uses the employer's resources (materials, supplies, time) to create a trade secret, invention or process.

As you can see, winning a shop right is often a hollow victory since the employee is free to use the trade secret to compete with you. In addition, you must file a lawsuit to prove you have a shop right since only a judge can ensure that a shop right exists. It's far better to get outright ownership by including the Employer Ownership Provisions in Section A in a signed agreement with the employee.

A shop right does provide some benefit if the employee patents the creation, ending its trade secret status. At that point you have the right to use the innovation without infringing the employee's patent.

> **EXAMPLE:** A consultant for a power company was hired to install and maintain an electrostatic precipitator. However, the power company was not happy with the operation of the device. The consultant, observing the problems, conceived of an innovation that would detect particles of ash. The power company installed the device at several locations and the consultant, who later acquired a patent, sued for infringement. A federal court ruled that the power company had a shop right since the consultant had developed the innovation while working at the power company and using the company's resources. *McElmurry v. Arkansas Power & Light Co.,* 995 F.2d 1576 (CAFC 1993).

3. Copyrights

Even without a written agreement, an employer always owns copyrightable works—for example, software programs, books, artwork and music—that are created by an employee within the scope of the employment. These works are called "works made for hire," and the employer is considered the author of the work. The copyright lasts for 95 years from publication or 120 years from creation, whichever is shorter. (17 USC § 101.) So you can always make the material in a copyrightable work the subject of an NDA because it belongs to the company even if created by an employee.

> **EXAMPLE:** Jim is employed by a motion picture company to create software code that is used for special effects. The code is a trade secret and can also be protected by copyright. Since the motion picture company owns the copyright it can prevent Jim from reproducing the code in any software he may later write for another employer.

If a copyrightable work were not within the scope of employment, the employee would own it.

> **EXAMPLE:** Jim, the special effects programmer, writes a novel during his vacation. Jim owns the copyright in the novel.

The rules for acquiring copyright ownership from independent contractors are different from those that apply to employees; we discuss those differences in Section C.

C. Trade Secrets Created by Independent Contractors

A worker's status—that is, employee or independent contractor—makes a difference for determining ownership of intellectual property. But the solution is the same: You should have independent contractors who work for your company sign an agreement that transfers all trade secrets to the company. That way you can protect the trade secrets with an NDA.

Employee or Independent Contractor?

A number of laws govern whether a worker is an independent contractor or an employee, and each of these laws has a different way of looking at the issue. The IRS is probably the most important agency to satisfy when it comes to classifying a worker as an contractor. Under the IRS's test, workers are considered employees if the company they work for has the right to direct and control the way they work—including the details of when, where and how the job is accomplished. In contrast, the IRS considers workers independent contractors if the company they work for does not manage how they work, except to accept or reject their final results. In making its determination, the IRS looks at a number of factors, including whether a worker:

- is paid by the job or by the hour
- furnishes the tools and materials needed to do the work
- sets his or her own working hours
- is told in what sequence or order to work by the hiring company
- receives training from the hiring company
- works full-time for the hiring company
- works for more than one company at a time
- invests in his own equipment and facilities
- pays his own business and traveling expenses
- hires and pays assistants
- provides regular oral or written progress reports to the hiring company, or
- provides services that are an integral part of the hiring company's day-to-day operations.

To make sure you'll own any trade secrets created by an independent contractor, use a written agreement similar to the sample one, below. As you can see, we have included the standard nondisclosure language from Chapter 3 in this agreement so it serves as an agreement that guarantees your ownership of contractor-created trade secrets as well as an NDA.

If you are unsure whether a worker is an employee or independent contractor or are interested in independent contractor agreements that deal with additional issues, consult Working for Yourself: Law & Taxes for Consultants, Freelancers & Independent Contractors *by Attorney Stephen Fishman (Nolo).*

This agreement may be found on the CD-ROM at the back of the book under the file name: ICAgreement.rtf.

Independent Contractor Agreement

This Agreement (the "Agreement") is made between _____
("Company"), and _____ ("Contractor").

Services. Contractor agrees to perform the following services:

_____

The services shall be completed by the following date: _____

During the process, Contractor shall keep the Company informed of work in progress.

Payment. Company agrees to pay Contractor as follows:

$_____ for the services and acquisition of the rights provided below.

Assignment, Works Made for Hire. Contractor assigns to Company any trade secret,
process, system, trademarks or patentable creation (Innovations) created by or discovered or
developed in whole or in part by Contractor as a result of any work performed by Contractor
under this Agreement. Such Innovations shall be the sole and exclusive property of
Company. Any works of authorship ("Works") commissioned pursuant to this Agreement
shall be considered as works made for hire as that term is defined under U.S. copyright law.
To the extent that any Works do not qualify as a work made for hire, Contractor hereby
assigns and transfers to Company all rights in such Works.

Contractor agrees to sign and deliver to Company (either during or subsequent to
commencing work) such documents as Company considers desirable to evidence: (1) the
assignment to Company of all rights of Contractor, if any, in any such Innovation or Work,
and (2) Company's ownership of such Innovations and Works.

Power of Attorney. In the event Company is unable to secure Contractor's signature on any
document necessary to apply for, prosecute, obtain or enforce any legal right or protection
relating to any Innovation or Works referred to above, Contractor irrevocably designates
and appoints Company (and each of its duly authorized officers and agents) as his agent
and attorney-in-fact, to act for and in his behalf and to execute and file any such document
and to do all other lawfully permitted acts to further the prosecution, issuance and
enforcement of patents, copyrights or other rights.

Contractor Warranties. Contractor warrants that any Innovations or Works created by
Contractor shall not infringe any intellectual property rights or violate any laws.

Confidential Information. For purposes of this Agreement, "Confidential Information" shall include all information or material that has or could have commercial value or other utility in the business in which Company is engaged. If Confidential Information is in written form, Company shall label or stamp the materials with the word "Confidential" or some similar warning. If Confidential Information is transmitted orally, Company shall promptly provide a writing indicating that such oral communication constituted Confidential Information.

Contractor's obligations not to disclose Confidential Information do not extend to information that is: (a) publicly known at the time of disclosure under this Agreement or subsequently becomes publicly known through no fault of Contractor; (b) discovered or created by Contractor prior to disclosure by Company; (c) otherwise learned by Contractor through legitimate means other than from Company or Company's representatives; or (d) is disclosed by Contractor with Company's prior written approval.

Contractor shall hold and maintain the Confidential Information of Company in strictest confidence for the sole and exclusive benefit of Company. Contractor shall carefully restrict access to Confidential Information to employees, contractors and third parties as is reasonably required and only to persons subject to nondisclosure restrictions at least as protective as those set forth in this Agreement. Contractor shall not, without prior written approval of Company, use for Contractor's own benefit, publish, copy, or otherwise disclose to others, or permit the use by others for their benefit or to the detriment of Company, any Confidential Information. Contractor shall return to Company any and all records, notes, and other written, printed, or tangible materials in its possession pertaining to Confidential Information immediately if Company requests it in writing.

The nondisclosure and confidentiality provisions of this Agreement shall survive the termination of any relationship between Company and Contractor except that this Agreement and Contractor's duty to hold Company's Confidential Information in confidence shall remain in effect until the Confidential Information no longer qualifies as a trade secret or until Company sends Contractor written notice releasing Contractor from this Agreement, whichever occurs first.

Relationships. Nothing contained in this Agreement shall be deemed to constitute either party a partner, joint venturer or employee of the other party for any purpose.

Severability. If a court finds any provision of this Agreement invalid or unenforceable, the remainder of this Agreement shall be interpreted so as best to effect the intent of the parties.

Integration. This Agreement expresses the complete understanding of the parties with respect to the subject matter and supersedes all prior proposals, agreements, representations and understandings. This Agreement may not be amended except in a writing signed by both parties.

Waiver. The failure to exercise any right provided in this Agreement shall not be a waiver of prior or subsequent rights.

This Agreement and each party's obligations shall be binding on the representatives, assigns and successors of such party. Each party has signed this Agreement through its authorized representative.

Contractor:

_____
(Signature)

_____
(Typed or Printed Name)

Date: _____

Company:

_____
(Signature)

_____
(Typed or Printed Name)

Date: _____

Here are instructions for preparing an agreement. First insert the names of the parties and indicate whether each one is a corporation, partnership, sole proprietorship or limited liability corporation.

a. Services

In the services section, insert the work that is to be performed—for example "Build and test prototype of solar-powered toothbrush" or "Compile demographic data about Republican dentists." If necessary, write "See Attachment A" and include a document labeled Attachment A in which the work is described more specifically. Insert the date of completion.

b. Payment

Insert the amount of payment. If the payment arrangement is more complex—for example, payments are contingent on performance goals—write "See Attachment A," and in Attachment A describe the payments more specifically.

c. Assignment, Works Made for Hire

You will notice that there is a special twist for copyrights. This language says that the company owns anything that qualifies as a work for hire (only certain categories of works qualify when created by an independent contractor (see "Enumerated Categories for Works Made for Hire," below); and that the contractor assigns to the company anything that does not qualify. This should take care of everything. In general, it's preferable for the company to acquire ownership of a copyrightable work under "work made for hire" principles instead of an assignment. That's because an assignment can be terminated after 35 years, while you will own a work made for hire for the length of the copyright.

Enumerated Categories for Works Made for Hire

To qualify as a commissioned work made for hire, the work must be used in one the following categories:

(1) as a contribution to a collective work;

(2) as a part of a motion picture or other audiovisual work;

(3) as a translation;

(4) as a supplementary work (i.e., a work prepared for publication as a supplement to a work by another author for the purpose of introducing, concluding, illustrating, explaining, revising, commenting upon, or assisting in the use of the other work, such as forewords, afterwords, pictorial illustrations, maps, charts, tables, editorial notes, musical arrangements, answer material for tests, bibliographies, appendixes, and indexes);

(5) as a compilation;

(6) as an instructional text (An instructional text is a literary, pictorial, or graphic work prepared for use in day-to-day instructional activities. For example, a textbook would be an instructional text, but a novel used in a literature class would not);

(7) as a test or as answer material for a test; or

(8) as an atlas.

These enumerated categories only apply to works created by independent contractors. Any work created by an employee (as defined in the preceding sections) is a work made for hire, regardless of the category.

d. Contractor Warranties

Here the independent contractor promises that the work will not infringe any other intellectual property. If another company sues you claiming that the contractor used its intellectual property, this gives you the right to sue the contractor for breaking the promise.

e. Confidential Information

As you can see, this provision establishes basic nondisclosure requirements. For an explanation, review Chapter 3.

f. Miscellaneous

Explanations for these miscellaneous provisions can be found in Chapter 3. In addition, you can insert other contract provisions—for example, arbitration, mediation or injunctive relief—if you wish. Examples of these provisions and explanations for their use are provided in Chapter 3.

 If you are concerned about issues relating to the joint ownership of trade secrets—for example, your company and another share ownership—detailed joint ownership agreements dealing with patents and trade secrets can be found in License Your Invention *by attorney Richard Stim (Nolo).*

D. Transferring Trade Secret Ownership to (or From) Your Business

If you want to sell a trade secret (in return for a lump sum or royalties), or acquire one from another company, an employee or contractor, you need a document called an assignment. An assignment is a permanent transfer, like the sale of a house, after which the seller no longer has any rights over the property.

An Assignment vs. a License

An assignment differs from a license, in which a company permits another to use its trade secrets in return for payments. Under a license, a company retains ownership of the trade secret. In some cases, a license has the same effect as an assignment. This is true in the case of an unlimited exclusive license, in which the company buying the license obtains the sole right to market the confidential information for an unlimited period of time. The seller is not keeping any rights that could be made the subject of another license, so the license really has the same effect as an assignment. Because the two terms may overlap, it's always important to examine the specific conditions and obligations of each agreement rather than simply to rely on the titles assignment or license.

Below are some examples of when you will need an assignment:

- You create and own a trade secret as a sole proprietor and later change your business form to corporation, general partnership, limited partnership or limited liability company. You should assign your trade secret to the new business.
- A competitor is folding and you intend to purchase its trade secrets.
- You want to buy a trade secret that is owned by an independent contractor or employee.

A basic sample assignment is provided below. Instructions for using it follow the sample agreement.

This assignment agreement may be found on the CD-ROM at the back of the book under the file name: IntelPropAssign.rtf.

If you are selling trade secrets, avoid doing it for the promise of future payments. Always try to get the money before signing the assignment. That's because if the person who owes you the money fails to pay you, you will be trapped in litigation, fighting to get your trade secret back. If you do agree to a series of payments, there are several solutions such as establishing an escrow account, transferring partial assignments as each payment is made, or setting up a license agreement that allows for ownership transfer after the final payment. Consult an attorney to best protect your interests.

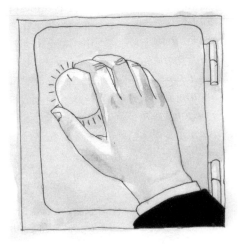

Assignment of Intellectual Property Rights

_____ [*insert name of person or company assigning rights*] ("Assignor") is the owner of all proprietary and intellectual property rights, including trade secrets, copyrights and patents, in the concepts and technologies known as _____ [*insert titles that describe the properties being transferred*] and more specifically described in Attachment A [*attach a description of the confidential information to the Assignment and label it "Attachment A"*] to this Assignment (and referred to collectively as the "Properties") and the right to registrations to the Properties; and _____ [*insert name of person or company to whom rights will be assigned,*] ("Assignee") desires to acquire the ownership of all proprietary rights, including, but not limited to the copyrights, trade secrets, trademarks and associated goodwill and patent rights in the Properties and the registrations to the Properties;

Therefore, for valuable consideration, the receipt of which is acknowledged, Assignor assigns to Assignee ___% [*insert percentage of interest that is being assigned—it can be less than 100%*] of all rights, title and interest in the Properties, including:

(1) all copyrights, trade secrets, trademarks and associated good will and all patents which may be granted on the Properties;

(2) all applications for patents (including divisions, continuations in whole or part or substitute applications) in the United States or any foreign countries whose duty it is to issue such patents;

(3) any reissues and extensions of such patents; and

(4) all priority rights under the International Convention for the Protection of Industrial Property for every member country.

Assignor warrants that: (1) Assignor is the legal owner of all rights, title and interest in the Properties; (2) that such rights have not been previously licensed, pledged, assigned, or encumbered; and (3) that this assignment does not infringe on the rights of any person. Assignor agrees to cooperate with Assignee and to execute and deliver all papers, instruments and assignments as may be necessary to vest all right, title and interest in and to the intellectual property rights to the Properties in Assignor. Assignor further agrees to testify in any legal proceeding, sign all lawful papers and applications and make all rightful oaths and generally do everything possible to aid Assignee to obtain and enforce proper protection for the Properties in all countries.

Date: _____   Assignor _____

[*to be completed by notary public*]
[*Add Notarization*]

Explanation for Assignment of Intellectual Property Rights

This is an all-purpose assignment that will transfer all intellectual property rights to a trade secret. It is essential that the information be defined as accurately as possible, without destroying the secret. Describe its purpose and effect—for example, title your property "Method of Transmitting Map Data Using Wireless Technology" and in Exhibit A state: "The Property is a process in which data from various cartographic sources is sorted and reformulated for wireless telephone transmission. The process combines standard GPS principles with a novel data-sorting method that enables faster transmission of packets of information using WAP transmissions. Using the method, a user can achieve more accurate mapping information in one-quarter of the time of existing map transmission technologies." This defines the principles of the secret and its effect. The actual information required to implement the secret should be provided separately.

In the blank section for the new owner's (assignee's) interest, insert the percentage interest. You can assign any amount of the interest from 1 to 100% provided that the total of all of the owner percentages equals 100%.

The numbered list is a collection of all potential rights that may be embodied in the property. The statement that begins with "Assignor warrants … " is a promise by the party assigning rights that the property can be transferred without problems—that is, it was not taken from someone without permission, and the sale does not violate any laws. Although it is not mandatory that the assignor's signature be notarized, we strongly recommend it, particularly if the trade secret is likely to become the subject of a patent or copyright application. In these cases, notarization makes the assignment less likely to be subject to challenge by the person selling the secret. ■

If Someone Violates an NDA

What happens if someone who has signed an NDA steals one of your trade secrets? Unfortunately, enforcing an NDA usually requires hiring an attorney and filing a lawsuit, an unpleasant and expensive proposition. This chapter addresses that frightening prospect by providing information about your options.

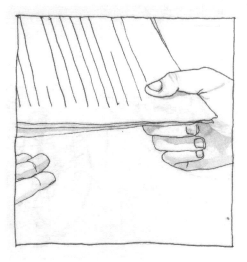

Even Without an NDA, the Law Is On Your Side

Whether or not you have an NDA, you can take legal action against the theft of your trade secrets, known as misappropriation, under state laws. Misappropriation is the acquisition or disclosure of trade secrets by improper means including theft, bribery and fraud. Examples include:

- A company promises a competitor's employee a better job in return for providing trade secrets.
- An employee furnishes trade secrets to a newspaper reporter.
- Key employees take confidential customer information and open a competing business.
- A hacker breaks into a company's computer network, downloads trade secret information and posts it on a website.

Most of the laws that protect trade secrets are based upon the Uniform Trade Secrets Act (UTSA). In Appendix A, we provide an explanation of these laws, as well as instructions on how you can research your state's trade secret law.

A. Four Steps to Take If an NDA Is Violated

Consider this scenario. You arrive at work and learn that the company email account has been hacked and secret files have been copied. You suspect a recently fired contractor who had signed an NDA. What do you do? If you suspect theft of trade secrets, we suggest taking the following steps.

1. Contact an Attorney

Battling over trade secrets, like hang-gliding, is a high-risk activity. An experienced attorney can minimize your risks, preserve your trade secret rights and provide a realistic perspective of your chances in the dispute. (Section F discusses hiring an attorney and keeping your legal costs down.)

Although your attorney will direct you in the remaining steps described in this section—acquiring evidence, determining injuries, proving trade secrecy and determining your legal claims—it's not wise or efficient to rely solely on your attorney. You must stay informed and take an active role in making litigation decisions. And to do that, become familiar with the risks and legal principles discussed in this chapter.

2. Acquire Evidence

Whenever trade secrets are lost—whether or not an NDA is violated—you will need to investigate, or hire an investigator, to learn as much as possible about the trade secrecy loss. These investigations commonly require surveillance of employees. Consult your attorney before hiring an investigator or using undercover surveillance because these actions may make you liable for claims such as invasion of privacy. Most investigations are performed surreptitiously because your employees may have ties to a former employee accused of trade secret theft and the presence of investigators may tip your hand.

Investigation of the theft is crucial. If you file a lawsuit and you don't have any evidence to prove your case, you can be ordered to pay the other side's attorney fees under the Uniform Trade Secrets Act (UTSA) or under an attorney fee provision in an NDA. Also, if you make public statements that contain unprovable accusations of trade secret theft and you injure that person's reputation, you may be liable for defamation.

Direct evidence of trade secret misappropriation is often hard to come by. If the dispute goes to trial, a court may infer misappropriation from ambiguous circumstantial evidence. For example, consider a former employee who signed an NDA and subsequently took a job with a competitor. Sufficient circumstantial evidence may be that: confidential information is missing from the former employee's office or computer; in an unusual departure of routine, the former employee worked late hours or on weekends; and the competing business has begun to use similar trade secret technology. When gathering evidence, you will need information about:

- The means of misappropriation. How did the secrets leave your business? Was information passed by email, diskettes or in conversations? You should inspect relevant company files to determine if any documents are missing. Examine computers used by current and ex-employees as well as email logs and telephone logs. As you may be aware, information stored on computers is not removed when it is deleted; remnants often remain that permit reconstruction of files. It may be possible to determine Internet use of computers (for example, which sites were visited by an employee) by examining logs kept by your company's Internet server or Internet service provider.

- Use of the trade secret. If you suspect that your stolen secret is being used in another company's product, acquire the product and, if possible, reverse engineer it to verify that the secret has been used.

- Who is involved in the chain of misappropriation? If possible, find out the name, address and business form (corporation, partnership, etc.) of anyone who may have had access to your secret—for example, an ex-employee, a competitor, or a go-be-

tween who may have arranged the transfer. This information will be needed if you sue or confront trade secret thieves. There are ways to obtain financial information about any of these parties in order to evaluate what you should sue for (money, a court order, or both). Your attorney can advise you how to acquire this data.

In addition, you should also gather evidence that your confidential information has economic value, is not generally known and is subject to reasonable security efforts. (Most of these attributes are discussed in Chapter 1.) You'll also have to document the origins of trade secrets and furnish copies of signed NDAs to your lawyer.

3. Determine What Legal Claims To Make

In order to put a halt to a disclosure—either through negotiation or litigation—your lawyer will need to show that you have solid grounds for a lawsuit against the person who violated the NDA. One legal claim you'll make is that the person has committed breach of contract. In addition, you and your attorney must determine whether you have other grounds on which to sue the perpetrators

Each one you come up with may provide you with a separate remedy and separate damages. Here are some possibilities:

- **Misappropriation of trade secrets.** When someone acquires or discloses your trade secrets by theft, bribery or fraud, you can sue under state trade secret laws for misappropriation. For more information, see Appendix A.

- **Breach of fiduciary duty**. Courts recognize that certain business relationships—for example, the relationships of executive officers or members of the board of directors to the company—require a higher than normal degree of trust between the parties. These relationships are referred to as "fiduciary relationships," and people or businesses in them are said to owe a duty of trust to each other. If that duty is breached, it may justify a separate legal claim.

- **Copyright infringement.** Trade secrets often include written, visual or other materials that are protected under copyright law. If the person who violated the NDA published, or distributed these materials, you may be able to claim copyright infringement (see Chapter 1).

- **Conversion.** Conversion occurs when someone, without authorization, deprives you of your use and possession of personal property (that's anything but real estate). For example, conversion occurs if a former employee takes a company's computer hard drive. It differs from theft, a crime that is prosecuted by government attorneys and may result in imprisonment.

- **Patent infringement.** Someone who violated an NDA may also have infringed a patent. Patent infringement occurs when someone sells, manufactures or uses a patented invention without authorization (see Chapter 1).

- **Trespass.** Trespass is the unauthorized entry on another person's real estate, for example, if someone breaks into your office. This differs from criminal trespass, a crime that may result in imprisonment.

- **RICO.** The Racketeer Influenced and Corrupt Organizations (RICO) Act allows someone to sue a person or business that engages in a pattern of criminal activity—for example, if a business steals your secrets and bribes your employees, you can sue the business for violation of RICO. Even though it involves criminal activity, a RICO claim is a civil claim and can result in an award of financial damages.

Criminal Prosecution

Several states and the federal government have passed laws that make the unauthorized disclosure, theft or use of a trade secret a crime. Under these laws the government, not private businesses, arrests the perpetrators and brings criminal charges. The penalties—including imprisonment—can be much more severe than in a civil suit. A person convicted of violating the federal Electronic Espionage Act of 1996 can be imprisoned up to 10 years.

The filing of a criminal case does not prevent you from suing. For example, in a case involving the Avery-Dennison company, a Taiwanese competitor was ordered to pay $5 million in fines to the government as a result of criminal charges and $60 million to Avery-Dennison as a result of a civil lawsuit involving claims of trade secret misappropriation, RICO violations and conversion.

Criminal prosecutions of trade secret theft are rare because many businesses prefer not to bring law enforcement officials into the fray. Also, in some cases, law enforcement officials don't wish to prosecute because there may not be sufficient evidence to obtain conviction. Keep in mind that the standards of proof for criminal cases are higher than for civil battles.

4. Determine What You Lost and What You Want

How has the trade secrecy loss affected your business? You need to know in order to figure out what you want from the perpetrators. For example, if you intended to patent an invention, disclosure of confidential information may ruin your chances.

In his treatise on trade secrets, attorney James Pooley describes three stages of trade secret misappropriation: threatened, continuing and completed. The extent of your injury, and the appropriate remedy, depend upon which stage you're at.

- A *threatened misappropriation* is one in which your confidential information has not been disclosed to the public or used by a competitor—for example, if you learn that an ex-employee was photocopying your company's trade secret material and will soon be starting work with a competitor. This type of problem is sometimes resolved by a written request to the employee to return all confidential materials. If that fails, you may need to quickly go to court for an order requiring the employee to return the materials and not disclose them.

- In a *continuing misappropriation,* an injury has occurred, but trade secret rights may not have been lost— for example, a competitor is using a secret of yours but has not publicly disclosed it. In this situation, you may be able to obtain a court order halting the unauthorized use and, in some cases, to receive compensation from the competitor. In this way your business can still retain trade secret rights.

- A *completed misappropriation* is one in which your injuries are extensive and irreversible. You can't reclaim trade secret rights because the secret has been publicly disclosed or extensively used by a competitor. In other words, a court order prohibiting continuing or future uses would not provide much benefit because the cat is out of the bag. The best remedy is to file a lawsuit and demand a financial payment from the competitor: either your lost profits or the competitor's profits. Or you might allow the competitor to continue using the secret and negotiate a continuing royalty.

As you can see, the extent of your injury also affects the speed with which you must take action. A threatened misappropriation requires immediate action; you must rush to obtain a court order preventing disclosure. The same immediacy is not present if the misappropriation is completed and the damage is done.

As with medical injuries, your course of action in a trade secret dispute is dictated by the available cures (or "remedies"). You need to figure out your remedies before your attorney sends a letter to the other party. These potential remedies can be used as leverage to end the dispute before a lawsuit is filed. Potential remedies include:

a. Injunctions

An injunction is a court order directed at those who have stolen your secrets. Asking for an injunction is common, since the primary goal of an NDA is to keep information secret.

Courts are authorized to issue emergency injunctions, called temporary restraining orders (TROs) in a matter of days, when you show that a trade secret is at risk of being lost as a result of the misappropriation. The court must then schedule a hearing at which all sides may be heard. If, after this hearing, the court still believes that a trade secret is at stake and that you will probably win at trial, it can issue a "preliminary" injunction. This order will continue to prevent further use or disclosure of the trade secret pending a final decision in the case. As a practical matter, once a preliminary injunction is granted, the parties often settle, rather than fight the case through to trial and beyond.

Sometimes injunctions are permanent —that is, they are final court orders in the case. More commonly, courts give the rightful owner of the trade secret a "head start" by prohibiting the information's use by the competitor for such period of time as the court decides it would have taken the competitor to independently develop the information.

If a court determines that an injunction would not be appropriate—for example, the competitor has already engaged in widespread use of your secret and has ruined your competitive advantage—the court can instead order your competitor to pay you a reasonable royalty for further use of the trade secret.

Injunctions and Free Speech

The First Amendment to the U.S. Constitution prohibits the government from placing restrictions on a person's freedom of speech. One exception to this rule is that a court may issue an injunction against the public disclosure—usually in the form of a publication—of trade secrets that have been obtained in violation of an NDA, for example, if an employee violates an NDA and gives trade secrets to a reporter. A court would weigh several factors when deciding whether or not to forbid the reporter from publishing the secrets. The court would consider the commercial interest in the trade secrets, the reporter's right to speak freely and the illegal behavior used to acquire the trade secrets.

b. Compensatory and punitive damages

If you suffer a financial loss as a result of a breach of an NDA, you may be able to get a court to award money damages to you. Your damages are measured by either:

- the profits a competitor earned by using the trade secret, or
- the profits you lost due to the improper trade secret leak.

If the person or company you're suing acted with spite or ill will or a disregard for the probable injury (defined as "willful and malicious"), courts in many states can impose punitive damages. These are damages awarded to you for the purpose of punishing the wrongdoer and providing an example to other would-be trade secret thieves.

EXAMPLE: A court awarded punitive damages when an executive who took trade secrets from his former employer also intentionally deleted the information from company computers and removed all traces of the technology from the company offices. This conduct led to a finding that the theft was willful and malicious. *Bond v. Polycycle, Inc.*, 732 A.2d 970 (1999).

In reality, courts often strike down any punitives that are too far out of sync with the actual damages. In most states that have adopted the UTSA, punitive damages are limited to twice the amount of proven actual damages. For example, if the compensatory damages were $10,000, the court could award only $20,000 in punitive damages (for a total award of $30,000).

c. Attorney fees

If your NDA includes an attorney fee provision (see Chapter 3), you can ask the court to direct the other party to pay your lawyer's bills if you prevail. If you settle the case, neither side has to pay the other (unless the attorney fee payment was negotiated as part of the settlement). Even if there is no attorney fee provision in an NDA, a court may require the other side to pay your attorney fees if it is engaged in "willful and malicious" misappropriation. This decision is up to the judge.

What to Do If You're Accused of Violating an NDA

If someone accuses you of violating an NDA, you should take a course of action similar to that described in Section A. Review your NDA, retain an attorney, investigate the trade secret, determine the facts and review the defenses, remedies and alternatives to litigation.

In addition, check your company's insurance coverage. Your comprehensive or commercial general liability (CGL) policy may pay your attorney costs for defending the suit. Coverage is often established in a provision known as "advertising injury." Some courts interpret this provision to require insurance companies to defend lawsuits in which the trade secrets relate to marketing information. Consult your attorney and notify your insurance company promptly.

B. The Cease-and-Desist Letter

Once you have completed your investigation and reviewed the potential remedies, it's time for your attorney to contact those persons who have breached the NDA or violated trade secret laws—for example a competitor who has bribed an ex-employee to breach the NDA. The first volley is a warning, sometimes referred to as a cease-and-desist letter, that accomplishes the following:

- informs the parties of the existence of the trade secret (without disclosing it) and provides evidence of the ownership of the trade secret,
- requests that the alleged misappropriation be stopped immediately and that all physical evidence of the trade secret be returned immediately. If the secret is being used in a commercial process or product, the letter requests a halt to any further commercialization of the product or process.
- may request payment or a royalty for past misappropriation. Alternatively, you may offer the company another option, to pay ongoing royalties and continue selling the product or process under an agreement known as a license.

You may get a letter back from the company, offering to discuss the issues or if the other company reasonably believes you're going to sue it for misappropriation, it may instead bring a lawsuit asking for "declaratory relief." It may ask the court to determine the validity of a nondisclosure agreement or of a trade secret and whether it has been misappropriated. However, if your letter did not threaten a lawsuit, but proposed resolving the dispute some other way—for example, by requesting arbitra-

tion or by granting a license—the company has no right to request declaratory judgment.

C. Resolving the Dispute

Your next goal is to resolve the dispute efficiently. The strategy you choose depends on the facts in your case, the terms of the NDA, the personalities of the people you're dealing with and the remedies that you are seeking (see Section A4). Below are four ways that trade secret disputes are resolved.

 Disputes over a company's trade secrets are often personal. It's upsetting when a formerly trusted employee violates a confidence. You can't ignore these feelings. But when it comes time to take action, we advise you to try to put aside personal issues, sort out the facts and chart a course that will provide a prompt and fair resolution.

1. Negotiation

Settlements can be reached at any time during a dispute—before, during or after litigation. Many trade secret settlements are made after a cease-and-desist letter has been mailed, while the threat of a lawsuit is looming. That's because businesses prefer to avoid the financial drain and unwanted publicity of litigating. In some cases, a settlement is made immediately after a lawsuit has been filed—when one party has called the other party's bluff.

court decides failure to disclose it would cause injustice or conceal a fraud, you will be required to disclose it. In order to preserve secrecy, the court will issue a protective order. This order prohibits the participants in the lawsuit from disclosing the secret, and it "seals" the court record pertaining to the trade secret, making it unavailable as a public document.

8. Going to Trial

During the trial, you attempt to prove the elements of your case through witnesses or with physical evidence such as documents. The witnesses for each side are questioned by the side that called them, and then cross-examined by attorneys for the opposing side. A trade secret lawsuit can be heard in front of a jury (if either party elects) or just in front of a judge. There are some issues that a jury is not permitted to decide. For example, a judge, not a jury will determine whether or not an NDA is valid. However, a jury can decide whether the NDA was breached and the extent of damages.

After the jury deliberates and issues a verdict, the verdict is confirmed by the judge and becomes a judgment that can be enforced by the winning party. On rare occasions, a judge who believes that the law and facts do not support the verdict will set aside or void the jury's verdict.

9. Appealing to a Higher Court

Either side can appeal the trial verdict. For example, you could appeal if you won the case but were unhappy with the amount of damages. In most states, a three-member panel of judges will review the trial court transcript and related documents to determine whether or not a legal error occurred. If the parties are not satisfied with the appellate court determination, the only other recourse is to ask the state's supreme court (or if appealing from a federal appellate court, the U.S. Supreme Court) to hear the case. Unlike other courts, those highest-level courts accept only the cases they feel are important.

F. Working With an Attorney

This section describe how to find an attorney and how to keep your attorney fees down.

1. Finding an Attorney

The best way to get a referral to a good lawyer is to talk to other people who have actually used a particular lawyer's services. The worst is to comb through advertisements or unscreened lists of lawyers provided by a local bar association or the phone company.

Local bar associations often maintain and advertise lawyer referral services. However, a lawyer can usually get on this list simply by volunteering. Very little (if any) screening is done to find out whether the lawyers are any good. Similarly, advertisements in the yellow pages, in newspapers, on television or online say nothing meaningful about a lawyer's skills or manner—just that he could afford to pay for the ad. In many states, lawyers can advertise any specialization they choose—even if they have never handled a case in that area of law.

If you are having difficulty locating an attorney knowledgeable about NDAs and trade secret law we suggest you consider the American Intellectual Property Law Association (AIPLA) (http://www.aipla.org) or the Intellectual Property Law Association of the American Bar Association (http://www.abanet.org).

2. Keeping Fees Down

Attorneys versed in trade secret law generally charge $200 to $300 per hour, and a full-blown trade secret lawsuit can run to hundreds or even thousands of hours' work, most of it before trial. Depending on the complexity of your case, you should expect to pay an initial retainer of $5,000 to $10,000. Attorneys rarely handle this type of dispute on a contingent fee (a fee which you would owe only if you won).

To Save Yourself a Lot of Money and Grief, Follow These Tips:

Keep it short. If you are paying your attorney on an hourly basis, keep your conversations short—the meter is always running. Avoid making several calls a day; instead consolidate your questions and ask them all in one conversation.

Get a fee agreement. We recommend that you get a written fee agreement when dealing with an attorney. Read it and understand your rights as a client. Make sure that your fee agreement gives you the right to an itemized statement along with the bill detailing the work done and time spent. Some state statutes and bar associations require a written fee agreement—for example, California requires that attorneys provide a written agreement when the fee will exceed $1000.

Review billings carefully. Your lawyer's bill should be clear. Do not accept summary billings such as the single phrase "litigation work" used to explain a block of time for which you are billed a great deal of money.

Watch out for hidden expenses. Find out what expenses you must cover. Watch out if your attorney wants to bill for services such as word processing or administrative services. This means you will be paying the secretary's salary. Also beware of fax and copying charges. Some firms charge clients per page for incoming and outgoing faxes.

Keep in mind, you can always fire your lawyer. (You're still obligated to pay outstanding bills, though.) If you don't respect and trust your attorney's professional abilities, you should find a new attorney. But switching attorneys is a nuisance, and you may lose time and money.

For more information on how to handle a dispute with your lawyer, see Nolo's eBook Mad at Your Lawyer *by attorney Tanya Starnes.* ■

Noncompetition Agreements

A noncompetition agreement (also known as a "noncompete" or "covenant not to compete") is a contract in which someone agrees not to compete with a company for a certain period of time. Noncompetition and nondisclosure agreements both have the same goal: to prevent a competitor from using valuable business information. The difference is that a nondisclosure prohibits disclosure to a competitor; a noncompete prohibits even working for a competitor or starting a competing business. In other words, the noncompete is broader and more heavy-handed in its approach. (So heavy-handed, in fact that some states restrict or prohibit them; see Section A2, below).

The advantage of a noncompete is that you don't have to be concerned about whether an ex-employee will use secrets at a new job, because the employee is barred from taking the new job.

In some cases, noncompetes and nondisclosure agreements complement each other. For example, an Internet business might use a noncompete agreement to prohibit ex-employees from working for competitors for a period of six months. After that the employees may work for a competitor but will still be prohibited, under the terms of a nondisclosure agreement, from disclosing trade secrets. The six-month noncompete period guarantees that short-term business strategies won't be compromised, while the nondisclosure agreement guarantees that fundamental long-term business information and methods won't be lost in subsequent years.

Many small business owners like to be perceived as a friend to employees. But employees may not see you in that light if you present a noncompete agreements for their signatures. If you're torn between a desire to be liked and a fear of competition, keep in mind that according to the National Federation of Independent Business, 50% of new competing businesses are started by ex-employees. Creating an equitable noncompete with reasonable restrictions may be the best method of protecting your business, your investors and the livelihood of your remaining employees.

In this chapter, we'll discuss when and how to use noncompete agreements. We'll also look at how to prevent ex-employees from trying to snare your clients or hire away your other employees, by using a document called a nonsolicitation agreement.

A. When to Use a Noncompete

As a general rule, use a noncompete only when it is necessary to protect your competitive interests and the restrictions are not unreasonably burdensome to the employee. Courts generally look on noncompetition clauses with disfavor, and in most states they will be enforced only if their terms serve a legitimate interest and if they are reasonably limited in scope and time. (Some states, such as California, won't enforce employee noncompete agreements at all. See Section A2.)

1. Legitimate Business Interest

The primary justification for using a noncompete agreement is to prevent trade secrets from being disclosed to competitors. Why not just use an NDA? NDAs deter most employees from disclosing secrets, but for key employees, an NDA is sometimes not enough.

For example, consider an executive with an intimate knowledge of the women's hair care market who leaves one company to work for a competitor. Despite the best intentions of the executive, it is almost inevitable that in her new job she will use some confidential knowledge from her previous employer. The loss of a key employee to a competitor poses such a substantial risk that a business cannot afford the difficult, time-consuming and expensive litigation necessary to obtain relief under an NDA. Rather than prove that the employee actually disclosed a trade secret, a noncompetition agreement prevents a competitor from bringing the ex-employee on board—at least for a short time. If the ex-employee challenged the noncompete in court, the court would view this as a legitimate basis for requiring a noncompete agreement. (For more on the inevitability of disclosing trade secrets, see box, *The Inevitable Disclosure Doctrine,* below.)

Don't use a noncompete to bully an employee into staying. If a dispute arises over a noncompete agreement and a judge must review it, the judge will probably start with a presumption that restricting an ex-employee's right to work is unfair. You will have the burden of proving that you had a valid business objective for using the agreement. If your motive is anything other than a true commitment to protecting the integrity of your business, a court will probably refuse to enforce your agreement (not to mention that you've got an unhappy ex-employee who knows your trade secrets). You will have wasted time and money and you won't have accomplished your goal.

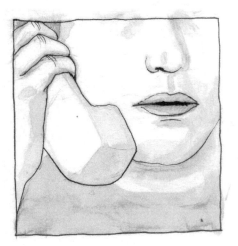

The Inevitable Disclosure Doctrine

Even without a noncompete agreement, a few businesses have been able to prevent certain ex-employees from working for a competitor under a legal concept—appropriately titled the inevitable disclosure doctrine. This principle was popularized by a 1995 case in which Pepsico successfully argued that a former executive could not help but rely on company secrets at his new job with a rival. *Pepsico, Inc. v. Redmond,* 54 F.3d 1262 (7th Cir. 1995).

Many legal experts have been dumbfounded by this rule since it allows a business to prevent an ex-employee from competing without the use of a noncompete agreement. From the employee's perspective, this rule is especially disturbing since it allows a former employer to get a court order preventing employment without any proof of actual or even threatened theft or disclosure of trade secrets. In other words, the rule is used to prohibit employment, not disclosure. *DoubleClick, Inc. v. Henderson,* 1997 N.Y. Misc. LEXI 577 (N.Y. Sup. Ct. 1997).

The use of the inevitable disclosure rule appears to be limited. Only a handful of courts have accepted it, and in many of the cases where it has been applied, the court has required more—for example, a showing of bad faith or underhanded dealing by the ex-employee.

2. State Law Restrictions

Noncompetition agreements can make it impossible for ex-employees to earn a living in their chosen line of work—a fundamental right. For this reason, some states will not enforce noncompetition agreements with employees or restrict how they may be used.

Summary of State Laws Affecting Noncompete Agreements

State	Code Section
Alabama	Ala. Code § 8-1-1
California	Cal. Bus. & Prof. Code §§ 16600-16602
Colorado	Colo. Rev. Stat. § 8-2-113
Florida	Fla. Stat. Ann, 542.33; 542.335
Louisiana	La. Rev. Stat. Ann. § 23.921
Montana	Mont. Rev. Code Ann. § 28-2-703
Nevada	Nev. Rev. Stat. Ann. § 613.200
North Dakota	N.D. Cent. Code § 9-08-66
Oklahoma	Okla. State. Tit. 15, §§ 217-219
Oregon	Or. Rev. Stat. § 653.295
South Dakota	S.D. Codified Laws Ann. §§ 53-9-8 to-11
Texas	Tex. Bus. & Com. Code. Ann. §15.03, 15.05

a. Alabama

Alabama prohibits "professionals," such as doctors and lawyers, from entering into noncompete agreements. Since the state courts have had a tough time assessing what qualifies as a profession as opposed to a trade or business, we recommend that you seek the help of an attorney if you want to create an agreement.

b. California

California refuses to enforce noncompete agreements between employers and employees. Employers in California should not use such agreements. To protect trade secrets, rely on nondisclosure agreements, which are enforceable in California.

Don't think that even though a court wouldn't enforce the agreement, you should have employees sign noncompetes anyway. It could cost you a lot. Learn from the example of Aetna, one of the country's largest insurance companies. It had a policy of requiring all of its employees above a certain level nationwide—including those in California—to sign noncompete agreements. Aetna knew noncompetes weren't enforceable in California, but believed that the agreements would be a "deterrent" to employees who were not knowledgeable about California law. When 25 California employees, including Anita Walia, refused to sign the noncompete agreement, Aetna fired them. Walia sued Aetna, and a jury awarded a $1.2 million verdict against Aetna. Not

long after this, Aetna stopped asking its California employees to sign noncompete agreements.

c. Colorado

Colorado prohibits anyone except "executive and management personnel and officers," as well as "employees who constitute professional staff to executive and management personnel" from entering into noncompete agreements with their employers. An employer in Colorado can enter into a noncompete agreement with any employee as long as the agreement provides only for the recovery of educational and training expenses if the employee violates the agreement. This recovery will be awarded only if the employee works for the employer for less than two years before switching to a competitor.

d. Florida

Florida law provides that a noncompete agreement can be used only to protect

- trade secrets or valuable, confidential business or professional information;
- relationships with specific prospective or existing customers, patients or clients; or
- extraordinary or specialized training.

The law also imposes time limits on such agreements. A noncompete agreement with a duration of six months to two years is assumed to be reasonable and enforceable. However, a noncompete agreement written to protect trade secrets can last up to five years.

e. Montana, North Dakota and Oklahoma

These states have statutes that appear to prohibit employee noncompete agreements. However, some courts in these states have indicated that, despite what the law says, noncompete agreements might be enforceable against employees if they are reasonable and necessary to prevent a former employee from disclosing trade secrets to a competitor.

 If you are located in one of these states, seek the help of an attorney to create an enforceable noncompetition agreement.

f. Oregon

Noncompete agreements are enforceable in Oregon if they:

- are entered into when employees are hired or promoted or
- qualify as a "bonus restriction agreement," in which case they can be entered into at any time during employment.

A bonus restriction agreement forces an employee to forfeit any profit-sharing or bonus compensation if the employee competes against the employer after the employee leaves the company.

Consult an Oregon attorney if you want to make this type of agreement.

g. South Dakota and Louisiana

South Dakota and Louisiana statutes allow noncompete agreements, but don't allow the agreements to last more than two years after an employee leaves the company.

h. Texas

Noncompetition agreements are usually enforceable against employees in Texas provided that the employer gives the employee a benefit in addition to the job itself as compensation for signing the noncompete agreement. The standards for such benefits are low—for example, granting the employee a fourteen-day notice period before the employee is terminated.

3. Nonsolicitation Agreements

A nonsolicitation agreement (also known as a "diversion" provision) restricts an ex-employee's ability to solicit your clients or employees. It doesn't prohibit an ex-employee from working for a competitor.

A nonsolicitation agreement complements an NDA because it prohibits the use of customer lists. For example, consider an interior designer whose ex-employee is hired by a local competitor. Rather than try to enforce an NDA, the interior designer can use the nonsolicitation agreement as a preemptive strike to prohibit the ex-employee from soliciting clients for a limited period of time.

Nonsolicitation restrictions are commonly included with noncompetition agreements, but you can use them separately. Courts in states that severely limit noncompete agreements or don't enforce them at all (see Section A2) generally enforce nonsolicitation agreements provided they don't:

- unfairly restrict an employee's ability to earn a living, or
- unfairly limit a competitor's ability to hire workers or solicit customers through legitimate means.

For example, an employee's agreement not to solicit an ex-employer's clients will probably not be enforced if the pool of potential clients is just four companies that use an obscure chemical. But if the customer pool is large enough to support reasonable competition, a court would enforce the nonsolicitation provision.

A sample nonsolicitation provision is in Section B3.

4. Using Noncompetes Intelligently

Noncompete agreements are a potential mine field. Many courts are averse to enforcing them and employees dislike being asked to sign them. In addition, there is a growing body of public information that helps employees break noncompete agreements (See for example, www.breakyournoncompete.com).

Reserve noncompetes for key employees—those persons with an intimate knowledge of your products, services, clients and customers. For example, a noncompete may be suitable for an executive who is privy to crucial business information, or an employee who creates your new products or marketing strategies— employees who could quickly provide a competitor with a substantial advantage.

In addition to avoiding indiscriminate use, you should make your noncompete reasonable in scope, time and territorial restrictions (see Section B2). In other words, it should be no more restrictive than necessary to protect your company's business.

B. How to Create an Enforceable Noncompetition Agreement

This section tells you how to create a reasonable, fair noncompetition agreement, one that will hold up in court if necessary. We also provide sample provisions that you can use with your employees. Below are examples of noncompete and nonsolicitation provisions that you can add to your standard NDA. Later in this section we provide a lengthier agreement that you can use to prevent disclosure, solicitation and competition.

 This agreement may be found on the CD-ROM at the back of the book under the file name: NoncompeteProv.rtf.

Noncompete Provision
(Can Be Added to Nondisclosure Agreement)

Employee agrees that in order to protect the Confidential Information while Employee is employed by Company, and for a period of_____ thereafter, Employee shall not:

(a) plan for, acquire any financial interest in or perform services for (as an employee, consultant, officer, director, independent contractor, principal, agent or otherwise) any business that would require Employee to use or disclose any Confidential Information; or

(b) perform services (as an employee, consultant, officer, director, independent contractor, principal, agent or otherwise) that are similar to Employee's current duties or responsibilities for any person or entity that, during the Term, engages in any business activity in which Company is then engaged or proposes to be engaged and that conducts its business in the following territory: _____.

This agreement may be found on the CD-ROM at the back of the book under the file name: NonsolicitProv.rtf.

Nonsolicitation Provision
(Can Be Added to Nondisclosure Agreement)

While Employee is employed by Company, and for a period of _____ thereafter, Employee shall not:

(a) employ, attempt to employ or solicit for employment by any other person or entity, any Company employees;

(b) encourage any consultant, independent contractor or any other person or entity to end their relationship or stop doing business with Company, or help any person or entity do so or attempt to do so;

(c) solicit or attempt to solicit or obtain business or trade from any of Company's current or prospective customers or clients or help any person or entity do so or attempt to do so; or

(d) obtain or attempt to obtain any Confidential Information for any purpose whatsoever except as required by Company to enable Employee to perform his or her job duties.

1. Give the Employee Something

Whether a promise not to compete is a stand-alone agreement or included in a nondisclosure agreement, the employee must be given something of value in return for signing it. Except in Texas (see Section A2), this is not a problem when a prospective employee signs the agreement before starting the job. The new job itself is considered an adequate benefit to make the agreement enforceable.

However, things are more complicated if you ask an existing employee to sign a noncompete agreement. In some states, keeping a job isn't considered enough of a benefit to the existing employee in return for signing a noncompete contract—which means that if the agreement were challenged in court, it wouldn't hold up.

Since state rules differ so much in this area, it is wise to provide a current employee with a clear additional benefit in return for signing a noncompete agreement. This is not difficult. Just link the signing of the noncompete agreement to some benefit—for example, an increase in salary not automatically mandated by the company, a promotion, additional vacation time or stock options.

2. Be Reasonable

Noncompetition agreements must be reasonable. If a dispute ends up in court, and the judge concludes the agreement is unreasonable, the court may refuse to enforce it at all or may ignore the unreasonable provisions and apply the rest. To be reasonable, a noncompetition clause must be limited as to time, scope and geographic region.

a. Time

A noncompetition agreement cannot last forever; it must have a definite time limit. The shorter it is, the more likely it will be enforced in court if there is ever a dispute. Such agreements typically last for no more than six months to two years. Unless you are convinced that a longer period is necessary to protect trade secrets, keep the noncompetition period to that time.

Some states have statutes that limit the time. In Louisiana and South Dakota, for example, noncompete agreements that last more than two years are presumed to be unreasonable. In New York, depending on the circumstances, restrictions from one to five years are considered reasonable. But even in states with mandated limits, courts can review and shorten noncompetition restrictions they deem unreasonable.

> **EXAMPLE:** A federal court in New York ruled that a one-year restriction on competition by a former employee was unreasonable because, given the dynamic nature of the Internet advertising industry, the useful life of the employee's information was much shorter than a year. *EarthWeb, Inc. v. Schlack,* 71 F. Supp. 2d 299 (S.D.N.Y. 1999).

b. Scope

A noncompetition agreement should be no more restrictive than necessary to accomplish your legitimate objectives. It cannot restrict an ex-employee from engaging in any and all business activities, since this would make it impossible for the employee to earn a living. Instead, the agreement should only restrict the employee from performing directly competing activities or those that might require the employee to disclose confidential information. The agreements in this chapter simply prevent a former employee from taking a similar position at a competing company or owning a competing company.

c. Territory

A noncompetition agreement should specify the geographic region in which it applies. Limit restrictions to the geographic area in which your company does business or in which it has made definite plans to do business in the immediate future. Anything broader than this would likely be deemed unreasonable by a court. Of course, if you market your products or services to customers throughout the United States—for example, if you operate an Internet retailer or a software company— your noncompetition agreement can apply to the entire country.

d. Optional provisions

Here are more ways that you can make a noncompete more reasonable:

- Permit the employee to work for a competitor if the employee can convince you that no confidential information will be disclosed to the new employer.
- Agree to pay all or part of the ex-employee's salary, at least for a while, if the employee is unable to find work because of the noncompetition agreement. For some companies, it may be worth it to prevent a key employee from working for the competition.

3. Sample Agreement

Below is an employee NDA that includes an obligation not to compete and an obligation not to solicit employees or customers. (Noncompetition and nonsolicitation provisions are commonly used together.)

This agreement can be used for someone who is about to start working for you (Alternative 1) or for a current employee (Alternative 2). If the agreement is used for a current employee, you must provide some kind of benefit to compensate the employee for signing. If you don't, the agreement will be unenforceable.

An explanation of the noncompetition and nonsolicitation sections is provided in Section A. Explanation for the remaining contract provisions are provided in Chapter 3.

 This agreement may be found on the CD-ROM at the back of the book under the file name: EmplNonAgreement.rtf.

Employee Noncompetition & Nonsolicitation Agreement

This agreement (the "Agreement") is entered into by and between
_____ ("Company") and _____ ("Employee")

1. Consideration

[Alternative 1]
In consideration of the commencement of Employee's employment with Company and the compensation that will be paid, Employee and Company agree as follows:

[Alternative 2]
In consideration of Employee's continued employment with Company and also in consideration of:

[Choose one]
❏ the amount of $_____

❏ options to purchase _____ shares of Company's stock

❏ _____

the receipt and sufficiency of which is acknowledged, the parties agree as follows:

2. Company's Confidential Information

In the performance of Employee's job duties with Company, Employee will be exposed to Company's Confidential Information. "Confidential Information" means information or material that is commercially valuable to Company and not generally known in the industry. This includes, but is not limited to:

(a) technical information concerning Company's products and services, including product know-how, formulas, designs, devices, diagrams, software code, test results, processes, inventions, research projects and product development, technical memoranda and correspondence;

(b) information concerning Company's business, including cost information, profits, sales information, accounting and unpublished financial information, business plans, markets and marketing methods, customer lists and customer information, purchasing techniques, supplier lists and supplier information and advertising strategies;

(c) information concerning Company's employees, including salaries, strengths, weaknesses and skills;

(d) information submitted by Company's customers, suppliers, employees, consultants or co-venture partners with Company for study, evaluation or use; and

(e) any other information not generally known to the public which, if misused or disclosed, could reasonably be expected to adversely affect Company's business.

3. Nondisclosure of Confidential Information

Employee shall keep Confidential Information, whether or not prepared or developed by Employee, in the strictest confidence. Employee will not disclose such secrets to anyone outside Company without Company's prior written consent. Nor will Employee make use of any Confidential Information for Employee's own purposes or the benefit of anyone other than Company.

However, Employee shall have no obligation to treat as confidential any information which:

(a) was in Employee's possession or known to Employee, without an obligation to keep it confidential, before such information was disclosed to Employee by Company;

(b) is or becomes public knowledge through a source other than Employee and through no fault of Employee; or

(c) is or becomes lawfully available to Employee from a source other than Company.

4. Noncompetition.

To protect the Confidential Information while Employee is employed by Company, and for a period of _____ thereafter, Employee shall not:

(a) plan for, acquire any financial interest in or perform services for (as an employee, consultant, officer, director, independent contractor, principal, agent or otherwise) any business that would require Employee to use or disclose any Confidential Information; or

(b) perform services (as an employee, consultant, officer, director, independent contractor, principal, agent or otherwise) that are similar to Employee's current duties or responsibilities for any person or entity that, during the Term, engages in any business activity in which Company is then engaged or proposes to be engaged and that conducts its business in the following territory: _____.

5. Nonsolicitation.

While Employee is employed by Company, and for a period of _____ thereafter, Employee shall not:

(a) employ, attempt to employ or solicit for employment by any other person or entity, any Company employees;

(b) encourage any consultant, independent contractor or any other person or entity to end their relationship or stop doing business with Company, or help any person or entity do so or attempt to do so;

(c) solicit or attempt to solicit or obtain business or trade from any of Company's current or prospective customers or clients or help any person or entity do so or attempt to do so; or

(d) obtain or attempt to obtain any Confidential Information for any purpose whatsoever except as required by Company to enable Employee to perform his or her job duties.

6. Confidential Information of Others

Employee will not disclose to Company, use in Company's business, or cause Company to use, any information or material that is a trade secret of others.

7. Return of Materials

When Employee's employment with Company ends, for whatever reason, Employee will promptly deliver to Company all originals and copies of all documents, records, software programs, media and other materials containing any Confidential Information. Employee will also return to Company all equipment, files, software programs and other personal property belonging to Company.

8. Confidentiality Obligation Survives Employment

Employee's obligation to maintain the confidentiality and security of Company's Confidential Information remains with Employee even after Employee's employment with Company ends and continues for so long as the Confidential Information remains a trade secret.

9. Enforcement

In the event of a breach or threatened breach of this Agreement, money damages would be an inadequate remedy and extremely difficult to measure. Company shall be entitled to an injunction to restrain Employee from such breach or threatened breach. Nothing in this

Agreement shall be construed as preventing Company from pursuing any remedy at law or in equity for any breach or threatened breach.

10. General Provisions

(a) Relationships: Nothing contained in this Agreement shall be deemed to make Employee a partner or joint venturer of Company for any purpose.

(b) Severability: If a court finds any provision of this Agreement invalid or unenforceable, the remainder of this Agreement shall be interpreted so as best to effect the intent of the parties.

(c) Integration: This Agreement expresses the complete understanding of the parties with respect to the subject matter and supersedes all prior proposals, agreements, representations and understandings. This Agreement may not be amended except in a writing signed by both Company and Employee.

(d) Waiver: The failure to exercise any right provided in this Agreement shall not be a waiver of prior or subsequent rights.

(e) Indemnity: Employee shall indemnify Company against any and all losses, damages, claims or expenses incurred or suffered by Company as a result of Employee's breach of this Agreement.

(f) Attorney Fees and Expenses: In a dispute arising out of or related to this Agreement, the prevailing party shall have the right to collect from the other party its reasonable attorney fees and costs and necessary expenditures.

(g) Governing Law. This Agreement shall be governed in accordance with the laws of the State of _____.

(h) Jurisdiction. In any dispute arising out of or under this Agreement, jurisdiction and venue of the dispute shall be federal and state courts located in _____ [*insert county and state in which parties agree to litigate*]. Employee waives any other venue to which Employee might be entitled by domicile or otherwise.

(i) Assignability: Employee may not assign or transfer rights or obligations pursuant to this Agreement without the prior written consent of Company. Any assignment or transfer in violation of this section shall be void.

(j) Successors: The rights and obligations under this Agreement shall survive the termination of Employee's service to Company in any capacity and shall inure to the benefit and shall be binding upon: (1) Employee's heirs and personal representatives, and (2) the successors and assigns of Company.

11. Signatures

Employee has carefully read and considered all clauses of this Agreement and agree that all of the restrictions set forth are fair and reasonably required to protect Company's interests. Employee has received a copy of this Agreement as signed by both parties.

Employee:

_____

(Signature)

_____

(Typed or Printed Name)

Date: _____

Company:

_____

(Signature)

_____

(Typed or Printed Name)

Date: _____

For examples of complete noncompetition agreements geared for employees and contractors, review How to Create a Noncompete Agreement *by attorney Shannon Miele (Nolo).* ∎

8

Other Ways to Protect Ideas

B y now you know how to protect your company's trade secrets using nondisclosure agreements. However, certain ideas—for example, a concept for a new product or a plot for a movie—may not meet the definition of a trade secret and may not be protected under the rules discussed in previous chapters. So what can you do if you want to submit one of these ideas to a company but fear being ripped off? Or if your company receives unsolicited ideas, and you're afraid of being sued by someone who claims you stole an idea?

The good news is that there are ways to protect yourself or your company. If you're submitting ideas, the best thing to do is to have an agreement, sometimes known as an evaluation or option agreement that demonstrates that the submission was solicited by the company for compensation.

> **EXAMPLE:** In 1983, two men submitted an idea to a movie studio—an African king comes to America, loses his memory, works in a restaurant, marries an American woman and returns with her to his kingdom. The men entered into an agreement that if the studio ever produced a movie based on the idea, they would be compensated from the film's profits. The studio made *Coming to America,* a movie based on the idea, which grossed over $300 million. The studio claimed it had no obligation to pay the men because the movie was not based on their idea.

The men sued and a court ruled in their favor because: (1) the movie studio had solicited the idea; (2) the parties had signed an agreement; and (3) $10,000 had been paid to the men when the idea was submitted. In the *Coming to America* case, no one factor was conclusive, but collectively these factors established that the idea submission was submitted in confidence and for economic benefit. *Buchwald v. Paramount,* 13 USPQ 2d 1497 (1990).

Below we review the factors that determine whether you will be compensated for submitting an idea. We also provide a sample agreement that can be used when you submit an idea for evaluation. If you are a company that receives unsolicited ideas, the rules in this chapter will help you fashion a policy for dealing with submissions.

A. How to Protect an Idea

Generally, when we talk of an idea, we're referring to a concept that has not yet been exploited and may not have economic value. For example, you may conceive of an idea for a television show, but unless you are in the business of producing television shows, the idea does not give you an advantage over competitors. The key to protecting these idea-submissions is to enter into an arrangement that respects the idea's potential value and justifies compensation.

Although the rules regarding protection of ideas vary from state to state, you can generally give yourself the maximum legal protection by following these principles:

- Maintain your idea with secrecy and use a nondisclosure agreement, and
- Don't submit it to a company unless it has been solicited and it is clear that the arrangement is for compensation.

Although we are assuming that your idea *isn't* a trade secret, it's also possible that it might be one. For that reason, we urge you to maintain it with confidence and obtain an NDA. This way, if the company to whom you submitted your idea refuses to pay for using the idea, you will be better positioned to argue to a judge that the material qualifies as a trade secret. (For more information on maintaining secrecy and nondisclosure, review Chapters 1 through 3.) That would be your first line of defense since, due to the vagaries of trade secret law, it is possible that the idea may qualify as a trade secret. If that argument fails you can still argue that it qualifies as an idea-submission, justifying compensation. That's where the second piece of advice comes in. You must be able to demonstrate that the company solicited the idea and agreed to compensate you for using it.

1. Don't Send Unsolicited Ideas

As a general rule, a company has no obligation to compensate someone for an unsolicited idea. Such ideas are like gifts given without strings attached. So if a company has not asked to see an idea, don't send it.

How do you get a company to ask? Usually, you'll need to solicit them first by letting them know you've got an idea. For example, "I've got a great idea for an improvement to your packaging—if you'd like to hear it, let me know." If the company responds with a letter or email, save it as evidence of solicitation. If a company rep calls and orally requests to see your idea, try to get some written evidence of the solicitation, even in the form of email. If you can't, make sure that your response addresses the fact that the idea was solicited. For example, "Dear Ms. Vogel: Per your request on May 14, I am sending you the patent drawings for my new invention." As you can imagine, it is often difficult to get a company to request an idea (see box, *"Getting Your Foot in the Door"*).

Sometimes a company may state that it is soliciting your idea "without obligation." Courts generally interpret this to mean that you are entitled to compensation if the idea is used.

EXAMPLE: A man contacted an automobile company and asked if the company was interested in seeing his idea. The automobile company requested the submission but stated that the request was "without obligation" on the company's part. A court interpreted this language to mean that the company was not obligated to use the idea but was obligated to pay if it did use the idea.

Getting Your Foot in the Door

It is rare that a company will respond to your letter and request to hear your ideas. Most companies are concerned that a submitted idea duplicates something that the company is already developing or that the idea is worthless but may result in a frivolous legal dispute. Here are some tips on overcoming hurdles you may encounter when presenting ideas to a company:

- A company may have a policy to consider an idea only if it can be protected under copyright or patent laws. In this case, the company has no obligation to compensate you for ideas that fall outside these categories. Submit only ideas that meet these legal standards—for example, a patent-pending invention or a detailed (and copyrightable) plot summary of a movie.

- A company may insist that you waive any right to sue over disclosures. In that situation, the company will be free to discuss or disclose the idea without your permission. This loss of secrecy places you in a vulnerable position—you could lose your idea.

You should seek the advice of an attorney before proceeding.

- A company may state that it has no obligation to return materials submitted with the idea. In this case, use common sense and don't send one-of-a-kind prototypes or materials that you cannot replace. ·

- If there is to be any compensation for the idea, a company may demand the sole right to determine the amount and method of payment. This take-it-or-leave-it approach poses a financial risk since there will be no negotiations for your compensation. If possible, solicit advice from others who have dealt with this company or other businesses in this industry before proceeding. If in doubt, consult an attorney before proceeding.

- A company may request that you waive all rights to sue the company regarding the idea. This is obviously risky—you won't have any recourse if you later believe your idea has been stolen. Consult an attorney before proceeding.

- A company may claim it has no obligation to compensate you if it is developing a product or service similar to the submitted idea. This is not uncommon—but get an attorney's advice before proceeding.

2. Make Sure the Company Knows You Mean Business

Don't send an idea to a company unless it is clear that the submission is a business proposition. All you need is to include a statement at the end of your letter something like, "I am sending this idea to you in the hopes that we can enter into a business relationship to exploit my submission."

> **EXAMPLE:** A man developed a ratchet by combining parts of two existing tools and brought it to the attention of an independent dealer for a tool company. Later, the man submitted a tool suggestion form to the company's corporate headquarters. The man did not request confidentiality and did not indicate that he expected compensation for his idea. The company manufactured and sold the ratchet without paying him. He sued, but the court ruled against him because he disclosed the information without stating that it was a business proposition for which he hoped to be paid.

3. Get a Written Agreement

You are more likely to be paid for your idea if there is a written agreement providing for compensation. (A sample agreement is provided in Section B.) The agreement states that the company solicited the idea as a business proposition and that the parties consider the idea to have economic value. An agreement can also establish that

the parties consider themselves to be in a confidential relationship. As we mentioned, it is sometimes unclear whether an idea is protected under trade secret law. In case your idea is legally a trade secret, we recommend you always include a statement that the submission is made in confidence.

4. Make Sure Your Idea Is Novel

Keep in mind that although an agreement creates an important presumption that you should be compensated if the company uses your idea, it does not provide complete protection. If the idea you submit is not novel—that is, it would be obvious to the company or perhaps to others in the industry—your agreement may be invalid as a matter of law.

That's because each party to a contract must contribute something of value. If the submitted idea has no novelty, it has no value, and therefore the contract is invalid. *Nadel v. Play-by-Play Toys & Novelties, Inc.*, 208 F.3d 368 (S.D.N.Y. 1999).

> **EXAMPLE:** A cross-marketing idea was submitted to a toy company and the National Basketball Association; the two entities would jointly market a Cabbage Patch Doll dressed in a basketball uniform. A court later determined that the company submitting the idea had no rights to compensation because the idea was obvious to the parties. *Khreativity Unlimited v. Mattel, Inc.*, S.D.N.Y., No. 99-9321 (SAS), 5/23/00.

5. If You Don't Have an Agreement

Even if the company doesn't sign an agreement with you, you may still be able to wangle some compensation for the use of your idea. Under limited circumstances, the originator and proprietor of an idea may stop others from misappropriating the idea if there was a "fiduciary relationship" between the parties and the idea was not generally known. In a fiduciary relationship one person stands in a special relationship of trust, confidence or responsibility. Fiduciary relationships are often defined by statute or case law. For example, the relationship of an attorney to a client is a fiduciary relationship, and stealing a client's idea would be a breach of that relationship.

Equally important is whether the parties are in a confidential relationship. If the parties have agreed not to disclose the secret without authorization, a presumption is created that the idea has economic value and deserves compensation.

B. How to Create an Idea-Submission Agreement

Agreements to consider an idea are usually either evaluation agreements or option agreements. A basic evaluation agreement provides that an idea is being submitted to a company for evaluation and that if the company intends to use the idea, it will pay the creator. With an evaluation agreement, you are free to submit the idea to several companies at one time. We provide an example of a basic evaluation agreement below.

With an option agreement, the company usually pays something when the agreement is signed. This payment gives the company the exclusive right to consider the idea during a period of time—perhaps six months or a year—referred to as the "option period." If the company decides to proceed (referred to as "exercising its option"), you and the company sign another agreement, selling or licensing the idea. If the option is not exercised, you can keep the option payment and are free to take the idea somewhere else after the option period expires.

Why does a company pay for an option? Because it wants to be sure that you will not take your idea to anyone else during the option period. In other words, the company is paying to keep the idea away from others for a time. In Section 7, we provide an explanation of how to convert the evaluation agreement into an option agreement.

Get your license or sale agreement ready now. *If you are using this sample agreement as an option agreement, the most prudent approach is to attach the license or sale agreement that you will later use if the company exercises its option. For more information on license and sale agreements, see* License Your Invention *by Richard Stim (Nolo). These agreements may involve complex legal issues beyond the scope of this book, so we recommend that you consult an attorney.*

Evaluation Agreement

_____ ("Disclosing Party") and _____
("Evaluating Party") agree as follows:

1. The Submission. Disclosing Party wishes to have Evaluating Party examine and evaluate
a submission tentatively known as "_____" and more specifically described in
Attachment A to this Agreement (the "Submission") with an eye toward assisting in the
exploitation of any products, services or other commercial exploitation derived from materials
contained in the Submission.

2. Review and Evaluation. Evaluating Party wishes to review the Submission and consider
whether, in its opinion, the Submission can be marketed to the parties' mutual benefit. The
materials furnished by Disclosing Party shall be used by Evaluating Party solely to review or
evaluate the Submission. After evaluating the Submission, Evaluating Party will either offer to
enter into an agreement with Disclosing Party for exploitation of the idea or return the
Submission to Disclosing Party and agree not to market or participate in the marketing or
exploitation of any product or service described in or derived from the Submission.

3. Nonexclusivity. Disclosing Party retains the right to submit the Submission to others while
it is being evaluated by Evaluating Party.

4. Confidentiality. The materials submitted by Disclosing Party describing the Submission
constitute valuable confidential information of Disclosing Party. The loss or outside disclosure
of these materials or the information contained within them will harm Disclosing Party
economically. Evaluating Party agrees to hold the Submission confidential and will not
disclose it to any person other than its evaluators and other members of its staff who have
reason to view the Submission.

Evaluating Party shall exercise a high degree of care to safeguard these materials and the
information they contain from access or disclosure to all unauthorized persons. All applicable
rights to the Submission remain vested in Disclosing Party. The foregoing provisions apply
with equal force to any additional or supplemental submissions and other materials submitted
or to be submitted by Disclosing Party to Evaluating Party with respect to the same subject
matter of the Submission.

5. Relationships. Nothing contained in this Agreement shall be deemed to constitute either
party a partner, joint venturer or employee of the other party for any purpose.

6. Severability. If a court finds any provision of this Agreement invalid or unenforceable as applied to any circumstance, the remainder of this Agreement shall be interpreted so as best to effect the intent of the parties.

7. Integration. This Agreement expresses the complete understanding of the parties with respect to the subject matter and supersedes all prior proposals, agreements, representations and understandings. This Agreement may not be amended except in a writing signed by both parties.

8. Waiver. The failure to exercise any right provided in this Agreement shall not be a waiver of prior or subsequent rights.

This Agreement and each party's obligations shall be binding on the representatives, assigns and successors of each party. Each party has signed this Agreement through its authorized representative.

Disclosing Party:

_____

(Signature)

_____

(Typed or Printed Name)

Date: _____

Evaluating Party:

_____

(Signature)

_____

(Typed or Printed Name)

Date: _____

 This agreement may be found on the CD-ROM at the back of the book under the file name: EvalAgreement.rtf.

Here is how to complete the Idea-Submission Agreement:

1. Introductory Paragraph

Insert the names of the parties. If any of the parties are corporations or partnerships, indicate the correct business form— for example, "Musto Motors, a California general partnership."

2. The Submission

Insert a phrase describing the idea. On a separate sheet write a description of the idea and label it Attachment A, and attach it to the agreement.

3. Review and Evaluation

This section prohibits the company evaluating the submission from using it without entering into an agreement for payment. In other words, the company has two choices: enter into an agreement or don't use the idea. In some idea-submission agreements and in many option agreements, an additional agreement is attached, which the parties will sign if the company wants to use the idea. Sometimes only the basic business terms are attached. For example, you might attach a sheet that explains the percentage of profits or the per-unit payment due if the idea is used.

For more information on these agreements, we advise you to consult an attorney.

4. Nonexclusivity

This establishes that the arrangement is not exclusive and that you are free to show the idea to others. If the evaluating party wants the exclusive right to consider the idea, it may enter into an option agreement as described above.

5. Confidentiality

This paragraph establishes that you own the idea and any additional submissions and that they must be maintained in confidence.

6. Miscellaneous

For explanations of the clauses dealing with Relationships, Severability, Integration and Waiver, see Chapter 3.

7. Converting the Evaluation Agreement to an Option Agreement

To convert the Evaluation Agreement into an option agreement, you must remove Section 4 and substitute this additional language after the section entitled Review and Evaluation.

Option Agreement Provisions

Exclusive Option. Disclosing Party grants to Evaluating Party the exclusive option to enter into an agreement to use the Submission. Evaluating Party shall have_____ months from the date of execution of this Agreement (the "Option Period") to exercise its option for the Submission by signing an agreement incorporating the terms described below.

During the Option Period, Disclosing Party shall not offer or grant any third party any rights to the Submission that will interfere with the exercise of the option granted to Evaluating Party. Evaluating Party shall pay to Disclosing Party the nonrefundable sum of $_____. If Evaluating Party exercises its option, such payment shall be considered as an advance against future payments to Disclosing Party.

[*Alternative 1*]
The agreement to use the Submission shall be substantially similar to that in Attachment A to this Agreement.

[*Alternative 2*]
The agreement to use the Submission shall incorporate the terms set forth below. The parties, acting in good faith, shall use their best efforts to incorporate the terms into a final agreement.

_____

_____

_____

The "Exclusive Option" provision establishes that the option is exclusive—that is, you cannot option rights to another company. Insert the number of months that the evaluating party has to consider the idea. Insert the amount of the option payment. The option payment is nonrefundable, meaning the disclosing party does not have to return the money if the company doesn't exercise its option. However, the payment can be applied to future payments if the option is exercised.

As previously stated, we recommend either attaching a copy of a sample license or purchase agreement to the option agreement or stating the terms of the subsequent arrangement. Use Alternative 1 if you have prepared a license or sale agreement. Attach it to the agreement and label it Attachment A. Use Alternative 2 if you have not prepared a license or sale agreement. State the key business terms such as length of license, advances, royalty payments and territory. Review *License Your Invention* by attorney Richard Stim (Nolo) for more information on license terms. ■

Glossary

cease and desist letter A letter from the owner of a trade secret (or copyright, patent or trademark) that requests that alleged illegal activity be stopped immediately

clean room A method of developing proprietary material in which an isolated development team is monitored. The purpose is to provide evidence that similarities to others' works or products are due to legitimate constraints and not copying.

common law A system of legal rules derived from the precedents and principles established by court decisions.

copyright The legal right to exclude others, for a limited time, from copying, selling, performing, displaying or making derivative versions of a work of authorship such as a writing, music or artwork.

database Information of any type organized in a manner to facilitate its retrieval.

declaratory relief An order from a court sorting out the rights and legal obligations of the parties in the midst of an actual controversy.

diversity jurisdiction Federal courts' right to hear lawsuits based upon non-federal claims; parties must be from different states and the amount in controversy over $50,000.

Economic Espionage Act A law making it a federal crime to steal a trade secret or to receive or possess trade secret information knowing that it is stolen.

evaluation agreement A contract in which one party promises to submit an idea and the other party promises to evaluate it. After the evaluation, the evaluator will either enter into an agreement to exploit the idea or promise not to use or disclose the idea.

fiduciary relationship When one person stands in a special relationship of trust, confidence or responsibility to another.

generally known Information is generally known if it has been published or publicly displayed or is commonly used within an industry.

improper means The illegal acquisition of trade secrets through theft, bribery, misrepresentation, breach or inducement of a breach of a duty to maintain secrecy, or espionage through electronic or other means.

inevitable disclosure doctrine Under this court-made rule, adopted by only a few courts, a court can stop an ex-employee from working for a competitor if the former employer shows that the employee will "inevitably disclose" trade secrets of the former employer.

injunction A court order requiring that a party halt a particular activity. A court can issue an injunction at the end of a trial (a permanent injunction) or immediately, rather than wait for a trial (a preliminary injunction). Two factors are used when a court determines whether to grant a preliminary injunction: (1) Is the plaintiff (the party bringing the lawsuit) likely to succeed in the lawsuit? and (2) Will the plaintiff suffer irreparable harm if the injunction is not granted? The plaintiff may seek a temporary restraining order, which lasts only a few days or weeks. A temporary restraining order may be granted without notice to the infringer if it appears that immediate damage will result—for example, that evidence will be destroyed.

jurisdiction The authority of a court to hear a certain type of case.

know-how A particular kind of technical knowledge that may not be confidential but that is needed to accomplish a task.

license A contract giving written permission to use an invention, creative work, trade secret or trademark, in return for payment.

misappropriation The theft or illegal disclosure of trade secrets.

noncompetition agreement A contract in which a person or company agrees not to compete with the business of another company for a period of time.

nonsolicitation provision (also known as a "diversion provision) An agreement that restricts an ex-employee's ability to solicit clients or employees of the ex-employer.

option agreement An agreement in which one party pays the other for the opportunity to later exploit an innovation, idea or product.

patent A grant from a government that confers upon an inventor the right to exclude others from making, using, selling, importing, or offering an invention for sale for a fixed period of time.

readily ascertainable Information is readily ascertainable if it can be obtained legally within an industry, at a library or through publicly available reference sources.

reverse engineering Disassembly and examination of products that are available to the public.

trademark Any word, symbol, design, device, slogan or combination that identifies and distinguishes goods.

trade secret Any formula, pattern, device or compilation of information that is used in business, that is not generally known, and that gives the owner of the secret an opportunity to obtain an advantage over competitors who do not know or use it.

Uniform Trade Secrets Act (UTSA) An act created by lawyers, judges and scholars, and adopted by 43 states and the District of Columbia, in order to conform the trade secret rules of different states (see Appendix A).

work made for hire (1) A copyrightable work prepared by an employee within the scope of employment; or (2) A copyrightable work specially ordered or commissioned for use as a contribution to a collective work, as a part of a motion picture or other audiovisual work, as a translation, as a supplementary work, as a compilation, as an instructional text, as a test, as answer material for a test, or as an atlas, if the parties expressly agree in a written instrument signed by them that the work shall be considered a work made for hire. ■

Appendix A

Each state has laws that prohibit trade secret theft. Regardless of whether you use an NDA, you can sue under these laws to stop disclosures, and in some cases, obtain financial damages. Although it is always advisable to use an NDA, these state laws provide a second line of defense in the event trade secrets are stolen.

Forty-three states (listed in Section A) and the District of Columbia have trade secret laws adopted from the Uniform Trade Secrets Act (UTSA), a "model" act created by lawyers, judges and scholars in order to conform the rules of different states. Section B, below, provides the full text of the UTSA.

Courts in states that have not adopted the UTSA follow common law principles (derived from court decisions or state laws) that are similar to the general principles expressed in the UTSA.

We include the full text of the UTSA so that you can review the standards and definitions used by state courts when reviewing trade secret disputes. For example, the definitions for misappropriation and improper means in Section 1 establish a broad range of prohibited activities that allow you to pursue a trade secret thief even if you do not use an NDA. Each state may make minor variations to this act so check your state statute to verify the standards.

A. States That Have Adopted the UTSA

43 states and the District of Columbia have adopted the Uniform Trade Secrets Act.

States That Have Adopted the UTSA

Alabama	Ala. Code. §§ 8-27-1 et seq.
Alaska	Alaska Stat. §§ 45.50.910 et seq.
Arizona	Arizona R.S. § 44-401 et seq.
Arkansas	Ark. Stat. Ann. §§ 4-75-601 et seq.
California	Cal. Civ. Code §§ 3426 et seq.
Colorado	Col. Rev. Stat §§ 7-74-101
Connecticut	Conn. Genl. Stat. §§ 35-50 et seq.
Delaware	Del. Code Ann. Title 6 §§ 2001 et seq.
District of Columbia	D.C. Code Ann. §§ 48-501 et seq.
Florida	Fla. Stat Ann. §§ 688.001 et seq.
Georgia	Ga. C.A. § 10-1-760 et seq.

States That Have Adopted the UTSA, con't

Hawaii	Haw. Rev. Stat. §§ 482B-1 et seq.
Idaho	Idaho Code §§ 48-801 et seq.
Illinois	Ill. Ann. Stat. ch. 140 §§ 351-59
Indiana	Ind. Code. Ann. §§ 24-3-1
Iowa	1990 90 Acts, ch 1201 Section 550.1 et.seq.
Kansas	Kan. Stat. Ann. §§ 60-3320 et seq.
Kentucky	Ky. R.S. § 365.880 et seq.
Louisiana	La. Rev. Stat. Ann. §§ 51:1431 et seq.
Maine	M.R.S.A. Title 10 §§ 1541 et seq.
Maryland	Md. Com. L. Code §§ 11-1201 et seq.
Michigan	M.C.L.A. §§ 445.1901 to 445.1910
Minnesota	Minn. Stat Ann. §§ 325C.01 et seq.
Mississippi	M.C.A. § 75-26-1 et seq.
Missouri	Mo. Stat. §§ 417.450 to 417.467
Montana	Mont. Code Ann. §§ 30-14-401 et seq.
Nebraska	Neb. Rev. Stat. §§ 87-501 et seq.
Nevada	Nev. Rev. Stat. §§ 600A.010 et seq.
New Hampshire	N.H. R.S.A. § 350-B:1 et seq.
New Mexico	N.M. Stat. Ann.§§ 57-3A-1 et seq.
North Carolina	N.C. Gen. Stat. §§ 66-152 et seq.
North Dakota	N.D. Cent. Code §§ 47-25.1-01 et seq.
Ohio	R.C. § 1333.61 et seq.
Oklahoma	Okl. Genl. Laws §§ 6-41-1
Oregon	Or. Rev. Stat. §§ 646.461 et seq.
Rhode Island	R.I. Gen. Laws §§ 6-41-1 et seq.
South Carolina	S.C. C.A. § 39-8-1 et seq.
South Dakota	S.D. Cod. Laws §§ 37-29-1 et seq.
Utah	Utah Code Ann. §§ 13-24-1 et seq.
Vermont	Ch. 143 Section 4601 et. seq.
Virginia	Va. Code. Ann. §§ 59.1-336 et seq.
Washington	Wash. Rev. Code. Ann. §§ 19.108.010 et seq.
West Virginia	W. VA. Code. §§ 47-22-1 et seq.
Wisconsin	Wis. Stat. Ann. § 134.90

The following states protect trade secrets under unique state statutes or under the common law: Massachusetts, New Jersey, New York, Pennsylvania, Tennessee, Texas, and Wyoming.

B. Uniform Trade Secrets Act

§1. Definitions

As used in this Act, unless the context requires otherwise:

(1) **"Improper means"** includes theft, bribery, misrepresentation, breach or inducement of a breach of duty to maintain secrecy, or espionage through electronic or other means.

(2) **"Misappropriation "** means: (i) acquisition of a trade secret of another by a person who knows or has reason to know that the trade secret was acquired by improper means; or (ii) disclosure or use of a trade secret of another without express or implied consent by a person who (A) used improper means to acquire knowledge of the trade secret; or (B) at the time of disclosure or use knew or had reason to know that his knowledge of the trade secret was (I) derived from or through a person who has utilized improper means to acquire it; (II) acquired under circumstances giving rise to a duty to maintain its secrecy or limit its use; or (III) derived from or through a person who owed a duty to the person seeking relief to maintain its secrecy or limit its use; or (C) before a material change of his position, knew or had reason to know that it was a trade secret and that knowledge of it had been acquired by accident or mistake.

(3) **"Person"** means a natural person, corporation, business trust, estate, trust, partnership, association, joint venture, government, governmental subdivision or agency, or any other legal or commercial entity.

(4) **"Trade secret"** means information, including a formula, pattern, compilation, program device, method, technique, or process, that: (i) derives independent economic value, actual or potential, from not being generally known to, and not being readily ascertainable by proper means by, other persons who can obtain economic value from its disclosure or use, and (ii) is the subject of efforts that are reasonable under the circumstances to maintain its secrecy.

§2. Injunctive Relief

(a) Actual or threatened misappropriation may be enjoined. Upon application to the court an injunction shall be terminated when the trade secret has ceased to exist, but the injunction may be continued for an additional reasonable period of time in order to eliminate commercial advantage that otherwise would be derived from the misappropriation.

(b) In exceptional circumstances, an injunction may condition future use upon payment of a reasonable royalty for no longer than the period of time for which use could have been prohibited. Exceptional circumstances include, but are not limited to, a material and prejudicial change of position prior to acquiring knowledge or reason to know of misappropriation that renders a prohibitive injunction inequitable.

(c) In appropriate circumstances, affirmative acts to protect a trade secret may be compelled by court order.

§3. Damages

(a) Except to the extent that a material and prejudicial change of position prior to acquiring knowledge or reason to know of misappropriation renders a monetary recovery inequitable, a complainant is entitled to recover damages for misappropriation. Damages can include both the actual loss caused by misappropriation and the unjust enrichment caused by misappropriation that is not taken into account in computing actual loss. In lieu of damages measured by any other methods, the damages caused by misappropriation may be measured by imposition of liability for a reasonable royalty for a misappropriator's unauthorized disclosure or use of a trade secret.

(b) If willful and malicious misappropriation exists, the court may award exemplary damages in the amount not exceeding twice any award made under subsection (a).

§4. Attorney's Fees

If (i) a claim of misappropriation is made in bad faith, (ii) a motion to terminate an injunction is made or resisted in bad faith, or (iii) willful and malicious misappropriation exists, the court may award reasonable attorney's fees to the prevailing party.

§5. Preservation of Secrecy

In action under this Act, a court shall preserve the secrecy of an alleged trade secret by reasonable means, which may include granting protective orders in connection with discovery proceedings, holding in-camera hearings, sealing the records of the action, and ordering any person involved in the litigation not to disclose an alleged trade secret without prior court approval.

§6. Statute of Limitations

An action for misappropriation must be brought within 3 years after the misappropriation is discovered or by the exercise of reasonable diligence should have been discovered. For the purposes of this section, a continuing misappropriation constitutes a single claim.

§7. Effect on Other Law

(a) Except as provided in subsection (b), this [Act] displaces conflicting tort, restitutionary, and other law of this State providing civil remedies for misappropriation of a trade secret.

(b) This [Act] does not affect: (1) contractual remedies, whether or not based upon misappropriation of a trade secret; or (2) other civil remedies that are not based upon misappropriation of a trade secret; or (3) criminal remedies, whether or not based upon misappropriation of a trade secret.

§8. Uniformity of Application and Construction

This act shall be applied and construed to effectuate its general purpose to make uniform the law with respect to the subject of this Act among states enacting it.

§9. Short Title

This Act may be cited as the Uniform Trade Secrets Act.

§10. Severability

If any provision of this Act or its application to any person or circumstances is held invalid, the invalidity does not affect other provisions or applications of the Act which can be given effect without the invalid provision or application, and to this end the provisions of this Act are severable.

§11. Time of Taking Effect

This [Act] takes effect on _____, and does not apply to misappropriation occurring prior to the effective date. With respect to a continuing misappropriation that began prior to the effective date, the [Act] also does not apply to the continuing misappropriation that occurs after the effective date. ■

Appendix B

How to Use the CD-ROM

The tear-out forms in Appendix C are included on a CD-ROM in the back of the book. This CD-ROM, which can be used with Windows computers, installs files that can be opened, printed and edited using a word processor or other software. It is *not* a stand-alone software program. Please read this Appendix and the README.TXT file included on the CD-ROM for instructions on using the Forms CD.

Note to Mac users: This CD-ROM and its files should also work on Macintosh computers. Please note, however, that Nolo cannot provide technical support for non-Windows users.

How to View the README File

If you do not know how to view the file README.TXT, insert the Forms CD-ROM into your computer's CD-ROM drive and follow these instructions:

- Windows 9x, 2000 and ME: (1) On your PC's desktop, double-click the My Computer icon; (2) double-click the icon for the CD-ROM drive into which the Forms CD-ROM was inserted; (3) double-click the file README.TXT.
- Macintosh: (1) On your Mac desktop, double-click the icon for the CD-ROM that you inserted; (2) double-click on the file README.TXT.

While the README file is open, print it out by using the Print command in the File menu.

A. Installing the Form Files Onto Your Computer

Word processing forms that you can open, complete, print and save with your word processing program (see Section B, below) are contained on the CD-ROM. Before you can do anything with the files on the CD-ROM, you need to install them onto your hard disk. In accordance with U.S. copyright laws, remember that copies of the CD-ROM and its files are for your personal use only.

    Insert the Forms CD and do the following:

1. Windows 9x, 2000 and ME Users

Follow the instructions that appear on the screen. (If nothing happens when you insert the Forms CD-ROM, then (1) double-click the My Computer icon; (2) double-click the icon for the CD-ROM drive into which the Forms CD-ROM was inserted; and (3) double-click the file WELCOME.EXE.)

    By default, all the files are installed to the \Nondisclosure Agreement Forms folder in the \Program Files folder of your computer. A folder called "Nondisclosure Agreement Forms" is added to the "Programs" folder of the Start menu.

2. Macintosh Users

Step 1: If the "Nondisclosure Agreement CD" window is not open, open it by double-clicking the "Nondisclosure Agreement CD" icon.

Step 2: Select the "Nondisclosure Agreement Forms" folder icon.

Step 3: Drag and drop the folder icon onto the icon of your hard disk.

B. Using the Word Processing Files to Create Documents

This section concerns the files for forms that can be opened and edited with your word processing program.

    All word processing forms come in rich text format. These files have the extension ".RTF." For example, the form for the Acknowledgment of Obligations discussed in Chapter 2 is on the file Acknowledgment.RTF. All forms and their file names are listed at the beginning of Appendix C.

RTF files can be read by most recent word processing programs including all versions of MS Word for Windows and Macintosh, WordPad for Windows, and recent versions of WordPerfect for Windows and Macintosh.

To use a form from the CD to create your documents you must: (1) open a file in your word processor or text editor; (2) edit the form by filling in the required information; (3) print it out; (4) rename and save your revised file.

The following are general instructions on how to do this. However, each word processor uses different commands to open, format, save and print documents. Please read your word processor's manual for specific instructions on performing these tasks.

Do not call Nolo's technical support if you have questions on how to use your word processor.

Step 1: Opening a File

There are three ways to open the word processing files included on the CD-ROM after you have installed them onto your computer.

- Windows users can open a file by selecting its "shortcut" as follows: (1) Click the Windows "Start" button; (2) open the "Programs" folder; (3) open the "Nondisclosure Agreement Forms" subfolder; and (4) click on the shortcut to the form you want to work with.

- Both Windows and Macintosh users can open a file directly by double-clicking on it. Use My Computer or Windows Explorer (Windows 9x, 2000 or ME) or the Finder (Macintosh) to go to the folder you installed or copied the CD-ROM's files to. Then, double-click on the specific file you want to open.

- You can also open a file from within your word processor. To do this, you must first start your word processor. Then, go to the File menu and choose the Open command. This opens a dialog box where you will tell the program (1) the type of file you want to open (*.RTF); and (2) the location and name of the file (you will need to navigate through the directory tree to get to the folder on your hard disk where the CD's files have been installed). If these directions are unclear you will need to look through the manual for your word processing program—Nolo's technical support department will *not* be able to help you with the use of your word processing program.

Where Are the Files Installed?

Windows Users

- RTF files are installed by default to a folder named \Nondisclosure Agreement Forms in the \Program Files folder of your computer.

Macintosh Users

- RTF files are located in the "Nondisclosure Agreement Forms" folder.

Step 2: Editing Your Document

Fill in the appropriate information according to the instructions and sample agreements in the book. Underlines are used to indicate where you need to enter your information, frequently followed by instructions in brackets. *Be sure to delete the underlines and instructions from your edited document.* If you do not know how to use your word processor to edit a document, you will need to look through the manual for your word processing program—Nolo's technical support department will *not* be able to help you with the use of your word processing program.

Editing Forms That Have Optional or Alternative Text

The following selection is for optional/alternative text without check boxes.
Some of the forms have optional or alternate text:

- With optional text, you choose whether to include or exclude the given text.
- With alternative text, you select one alternative to include and exclude the other alternatives.

When editing these forms, we suggest you do the following:

Optional text

If you **don't want** to include optional text, just delete it from your document.

If you **do want** to include optional text, just leave it in your document.

In either case, delete the italicized instructions.

Alternative text

First delete all the alternatives that you do not want to include, then delete the italicized instructions.

OR

The following selection is for optional/alternative text with check boxes.
Some of the forms have check boxes before text. The check boxes indicate:

- Optional text, where you choose whether to include or exclude the given text.
- Alternative text, where you select one alternative to include and exclude the other alternatives.

If you are using the tear-out forms in Appendix C, you simply mark the appropriate box to make your choice.

If you are using the Forms CD, however, we recommend that instead of marking the check boxes, you do the following:

Optional text

If you **don't want** to include optional text, just delete it from your document.

If you **do want** to include optional text, just leave it in your document.

In either case, delete the check box itself as well as the italicized instructions that the text is optional.

Alternative text

First delete all the alternatives that you do not want to include.

Then delete the remaining check boxes, as well as the italicized instructions that you need to select one of the alternatives provided.

Step 3: Printing Out the Document

Use your word processor's or text editor's "Print" command to print out your document. If you do not know how to use your word processor to print a document, you will need to look through the manual for your word processing program—Nolo's technical support department will *not* be able to help you with the use of your word processing program.

Step 4: Saving Your Document

After filling in the form, use the "Save As" command to save and rename the file. Because all the files are "read-only" and you will not be able to use the "Save" command. This is for your protection. *If you save the file without renaming it, the underlines that indicate where you need to enter your information will be lost and you will not be able to create a new document with this file without recopying the original file from the CD-ROM.*

If you do not know how to use your word processor to save a document, you will need to look through the manual for your word processing program—Nolo's technical support department will *not* be able to help you with the use of your word processing program. ■

Appendix C

Forms and Agreements on CD-ROM

Chapter	Form	CD-ROM title
2	Acknowledgment of Obligations	Acknowledgment.rtf
2	Letter to New Employer	NewEmployer.rtf
3	Basic Nondisclosure Agreement	BasicNondisclose.rtf
3	Additional Contract Provisions	AddProvisions.rtf
4	Employee Nondisclosure Agreement	EmplNondisclose.rtf
4	Nondisclosure Agreement for Business Negotiations	BizNondisclose.rtf
4	Visitor Nondisclosure Agreement	VisitNondisclose.rtf
4	Interview Nondisclosure Agreement	InterNondisclose.rtf
4	Software Beta Tester Nondisclosure Agreement	BetaNondisclose.rtf
4	Nondisclosure Agreement for Licensee	Nondisclose.rtf
4	Student Nondisclosure Agreement	StudNondisclose.rtf
4	Customer List/Mailing List Nondisclosure Agreement	ListNondisclose.rtf
5	Sample Employer Ownership Provisions	EmplOwnProvisions.rtf

Chapter	Form	CD-ROM title
5	Independent Contractor Agreement	ICAgreement.rtf
5	Assignment of Intellectual Property Rights	IntelPropAssign.rtf
7	Noncompete Provision	NoncompeteProv.rtf
7	Nonsolicitation Provision	NonsolicitProv.rtf
7	Employee Noncompetition & Nonsolicitation Agreement	EmplNonAgreement.rtf
8	Evaluation Agreement	EvalAgreement.rtf
8	Option Agreement Provisions	OptionProv.rtf

Acknowledgment of Obligations

1. I acknowledge that during my employment with _____
I have received or been exposed to trade secrets of the Company including, but not limited to, the following: [Check applicable boxes]

❏ Financial data

❏ Price or costing data

❏ Customer and vendor lists

❏ Marketing plans and data

❏ Personnel data

❏ Technical information concerning Company research and development projects, including [Describe] _____

❏ Product design and specification data, including [Describe] _____

❏ Patent applications and disclosures, including [Describe] _____

❏ Product information, including [Describe] _____

❏ Other _____

2. I have read, signed and been furnished with a copy of my [Choose one] Employment/Non-disclosure Agreement with the Company. I have complied with and will continue to comply with all of the provisions of the Agreement, including my obligation to preserve as confidential all of the Company's trade secrets.

3. I do not have in my possession original documents, copies of them or any other thing containing Company trade secrets. I have not disclosed Company trade secrets to anyone not authorized by the Company to receive them.

4. I have returned to my supervisor all identification badges, keys and other access devices issued to me by the Company.

_____

(Signature)

_____

(Typed or Printed Name)

Date: _____

Letter to New Employer

_____

To Whom It May Concern:

We understand that _____ has decided to join your company. We would like to inform you of the following facts:

During his/her employment by the _____, _____ had access to our trade secrets including, but not limited to, _____ _____.

In connection with his/her employment, _____ signed an Employment Agreement in which he/she promised not to disclose or utilize any of our trade secrets without our permission. The Agreement remains in full force and effect.

At the time _____ left our company, he/she was informed of her continuing obligations under the Employment Agreement. He/She signed an acknowledgment of these obligations, a copy of which is enclosed.

We are confident that _____ intends to comply with his/her obligations and respect our trade secrets. We also trust that your company will not assign him/her to a position that might risk disclosure of our trade secrets.

If you have any questions regarding these matters, we will be happy to clarify them for you. In addition, if at any time you wish to know whether information provided you by _____ is a trade secret owned by us, we will be happy to work out a procedure for providing you with this information.

Very truly yours,

_____
(Signature)

_____
(Typed or Printed Name)

Title: _____

Basic Nondisclosure Agreement

This Nondisclosure Agreement (the "Agreement") is entered into by and between
_____ with its principal offices at _____,
("Disclosing Party") and _____, located at _____
("Receiving Party") for the purpose of preventing the unauthorized disclosure of Confidential Information as defined below. The parties agree to enter into a confidential relationship with respect to the disclosure of certain proprietary and confidential information ("Confidential Information").

1. Definition of Confidential Information. For purposes of this Agreement, "Confidential Information" shall include all information or material that has or could have commercial value or other utility in the business in which Disclosing Party is engaged. If Confidential Information is in written form, the Disclosing Party shall label or stamp the materials with the word "Confidential" or some similar warning. If Confidential Information is transmitted orally, the Disclosing Party shall promptly provide a writing indicating that such oral communication constituted Confidential Information.

2. Exclusions from Confidential Information. Receiving Party's obligations under this Agreement do not extend to information that is: (a) publicly known at the time of disclosure or subsequently becomes publicly known through no fault of the Receiving Party; (b) discovered or created by the Receiving Party before disclosure by Disclosing Party; (c) learned by the Receiving Party through legitimate means other than from the Disclosing Party or Disclosing Party's representatives; or (d) is disclosed by Receiving Party with Disclosing Party's prior written approval.

3. Obligations of Receiving Party. Receiving Party shall hold and maintain the Confidential Information in strictest confidence for the sole and exclusive benefit of the Disclosing Party. Receiving Party shall carefully restrict access to Confidential Information to employees, contractors and third parties as is reasonably required and shall require those persons to sign nondisclosure restrictions at least as protective as those in this Agreement. Receiving Party shall not, without prior written approval of Disclosing Party, use for Receiving Party's own benefit, publish, copy, or otherwise disclose to others, or permit the use by others for their benefit or to the detriment of Disclosing Party, any Confidential Information. Receiving Party shall return to Disclosing Party any and all records, notes, and other written, printed, or tangible materials in its possession pertaining to Confidential Information immediately if Disclosing Party requests it in writing.

4. Time Periods. The nondisclosure provisions of this Agreement shall survive the termination of this Agreement and Receiving Party's duty to hold Confidential Information in confidence shall remain in effect until the Confidential Information no longer qualifies as a trade secret or until Disclosing Party sends Receiving Party written notice releasing Receiving Party from this Agreement, whichever occurs first.

5. Relationships. Nothing contained in this Agreement shall be deemed to constitute either party a partner, joint venturer or employee of the other party for any purpose.

6. Severability. If a court finds any provision of this Agreement invalid or unenforceable, the remainder of this Agreement shall be interpreted so as best to effect the intent of the parties.

7. Integration. This Agreement expresses the complete understanding of the parties with respect to the subject matter and supersedes all prior proposals, agreements, representations and understandings. This Agreement may not be amended except in a writing signed by both parties.

8. Waiver. The failure to exercise any right provided in this Agreement shall not be a waiver of prior or subsequent rights.

This Agreement and each party's obligations shall be binding on the representatives, assigns and successors of such party. Each party has signed this Agreement through its authorized representative.

_____

(Signature)

_____

(Typed or Printed Name)

Date: _____

_____

(Signature)

_____

(Typed or Printed Name)

Date: _____

Additional Contract Provisions

Injunctive Relief

Receiving Party acknowledges that any misappropriation of any of the Confidential Information in violation of this Agreement may cause Disclosing Party irreparable harm, the amount of which may be difficult to ascertain, and therefore agrees that the Disclosing Party shall have the right to apply to a court of competent jurisdiction for an order enjoining any such further misappropriation and for such other relief as the Disclosing Party deems appropriate. This right of Disclosing Party is to be in addition to the remedies otherwise available to Disclosing Party.

Indemnity

Receiving Party agrees to indemnify the Disclosing Party against any and all losses, damages, claims or expenses incurred or suffered by the Disclosing Party as a result of the Receiving Party's breach of this Agreement.

Attorney Fees and Expenses

In a dispute arising out of or related to this Agreement, the prevailing party shall have the right to collect from the other party its reasonable attorney fees and costs and necessary expenditures.

Arbitration

If a dispute arises under or relating to this Agreement, the parties agree to submit the dispute to binding arbitration in the state of ___ [insert state in which parties agree to arbitrate] or another location mutually agreeable to the parties. The arbitration shall be conducted on a confidential basis pursuant to the Commercial Arbitration Rules of the American Arbitration Association. Any decision or award as a result of any such arbitration proceeding shall be in writing and shall provide an explanation for all conclusions of law and fact and shall include the assessment of costs, expenses and reasonable attorney fees. Any such arbitration shall be conducted by an arbitrator experienced in ___[insert industry experience required for arbitrator] and ____ [insert area of law that is at the subject of your dispute, for example, licensing law] law and shall include a written record of the arbitration hearing. The parties reserve the right to object to any individual who is employed by or affiliated with a competing organization or entity. An award of arbitration may be confirmed in a court of competent jurisdiction.

Mediation & Arbitration

The parties agree that any dispute or difference between them arising under this Agreement shall be settled first by a meeting of the parties attempting to confer and resolve the dispute in a good faith manner.

If the parties cannot resolve their dispute after conferring, any party may require the other to submit the matter to non-binding mediation, utilizing the services of an impartial professional mediator approved by both parties.

If the parties cannot come to an agreement following mediation, they will submit the matter to binding arbitration at a location mutually agreeable to the parties. The arbitration shall be conducted on a confidential basis under the Commercial Arbitration Rules of the American Arbitration Association. Any decision or award as a result of any such arbitration proceeding shall include the assessment of costs, expenses and reasonable attorney fees and shall include a written record of the proceedings and a written determination of the arbitrators. Absent an agreement to the contrary, any such arbitration shall be conducted by an arbitrator experienced in intellectual property law. The parties may object to any individual who is employed by or affiliated with a competing organization or entity. In the event of any such dispute or difference, either party may give to the other notice requiring that the matter be settled by arbitration. An award of arbitration shall be final and binding on the parties and may be confirmed in a court of competent jurisdiction.

Governing Law

This Agreement shall be governed in accordance with the laws of the State of
_____.

Jurisdiction

The parties consent to the exclusive jurisdiction and venue of the federal and state courts located in ____ [insert county and state in which parties agree to litigate] in any action arising out of or relating to this Agreement. The parties waive any other jurisdiction to which either party might be entitled by domicile or otherwise.

Successors & Assigns

This Agreement shall bind each party's heirs, successors and assigns. Disclosing Party may assign this Agreement to any party at any time. Receiving Party shall not assign any of its rights or obligations under this Agreement without Company's prior written consent. Any assignment or transfer in violation of this section shall be void.

Assignability—Consent Not Unreasonably Withheld

This Agreement shall bind each party's heirs, successors and assigns. Receiving Party may not assign or transfer its rights or obligations pursuant to this Agreement without the prior written consent of Disclosing Party. Such consent shall not be unreasonably withheld. Any assignment or transfer in violation of this section shall be void.

Assignability—Consent Not Needed for Affiliates Or New Owners

This Agreement shall bind each party's heirs, successors and assigns. Receiving Party may not assign or transfer its rights or obligations pursuant to this Agreement without the prior written consent of Disclosing Party. However, no consent is required for an assignment or transfer that occurs: (a) to an entity in which Receiving Party owns more than fifty percent of the assets; or (b) as part of a transfer of all or substantially all of the assets of Receiving Party to any party. Any assignment or transfer in violation of this Section shall be void.

Confidentiality Provision

(a) Confidential Information. The parties acknowledge that each may receive or have access to confidential information (the "Confidential Information"). For purposes of this Agreement, "Confidential Information" shall include all information or material that has or could have commercial value or other utility in the business in which the party part disclosing the information ("Disclosing Party") is engaged. In the event that Confidential Information is in written form, Disclosing Party shall label or stamp the materials with the word "Confidential" or some similar warning. In the event that Confidential Information is transmitted orally, the Disclosing Party shall promptly provide a writing indicating that such oral communication constituted Confidential Information.

(b) Exclusions from Confidential Information. The party receiving the Confidential Information ("Receiving Party) shall not be obligated to preserve the confidentiality of any information that is: (a) publicly known at the time of disclosure under this Agreement or subsequently becomes publicly known through no fault of Receiving Party; (b) discovered or created by Receiving Party prior to the time of disclosure by Disclosing Party; or (c) otherwise learned by Receiving Party through legitimate means other than from Disclosing Party or anyone connected with Disclosing Party.

(c) Obligations of Receiving Party. Receiving Party shall hold and maintain the Confidential Information of the other party in strictest confidence for the sole and exclusive benefit of Disclosing Party. Receiving Party shall carefully restrict access to any such Confidential Information to persons bound by this Agreement, only on a need-to-know basis. Receiving Party shall not, without prior written approval of Disclosing Party, use for Receiving Party's own benefit, publish, copy, or otherwise disclose to others, or permit the use by others for their benefit or to the detriment of Disclosing Party, any of the Confidential Information. The Receiving Party shall return to Disclosing Party any and all records, notes, and other written, printed, or tangible materials in its possession pertaining to the Confidential Information immediately on the written request of Disclosing Party.

(d) Time Period. This Agreement and Receiving Party's duty to hold Disclosing Party's Confidential Information in confidence shall remain in effect until _____ [*include year*].

(e) Survival. The nondisclosure provisions of this Agreement shall survive the termination of any relationship between Disclosing Party and Receiving Party.

Employee Nondisclosure Agreement

This agreement (the "Agreement") is entered into by _____ ("Company") and _____ ("Employee").

[Alternative 1]
In consideration of the commencement of Employee's employment with Company and the compensation that will be paid, Employee and Company agree as follows:

[Alternative 2]
In consideration of Employee's continued employment with Company and also in consideration of:

[Choose one]
❑ the amount of $ _____

❑ options to purchase _____ shares of Company's stock

❑ _____

the receipt and sufficiency of which is acknowledged, the parties agree as follows:

1. Company's Trade Secrets

In the performance of Employee's job duties with Company, Employee will be exposed to Company's Confidential Information. "Confidential Information" means information or material that is commercially valuable to Company and not generally known or readily ascertainable in the industry. This includes, but is not limited to:

(a) technical information concerning Company's products and services, including product know-how, formulas, designs, devices, diagrams, software code, test results, processes, inventions, research projects and product development, technical memoranda and correspondence;

(b) information concerning Company's business, including cost information, profits, sales information, accounting and unpublished financial information, business plans, markets and marketing methods, customer lists and customer information, purchasing techniques, supplier lists and supplier information and advertising strategies;

(c) information concerning Company's employees, including salaries, strengths, weaknesses and skills;

(d) information submitted by Company's customers, suppliers, employees, consultants or co-venture partners with Company for study, evaluation or use; and

(e) any other information not generally known to the public which, if misused or disclosed, could reasonably be expected to adversely affect Company's business.

2. Nondisclosure of Trade Secrets

Employee shall keep Company's Confidential Information, whether or not prepared or developed by Employee, in the strictest confidence. Employee will not disclose such information to anyone outside Company without Company's prior written consent. Nor will Employee make use of any Confidential Information for Employee's own purposes or the benefit of anyone other than Company.

However, Employee shall have no obligation to treat as confidential any information which:

(a) was in Employee's possession or known to Employee, without an obligation to keep it confidential, before such information was disclosed to Employee by Company;

(b) is or becomes public knowledge through a source other than Employee and through no fault of Employee; or

(c) is or becomes lawfully available to Employee from a source other than Company.

3. Confidential Information of Others

Employee will not disclose to Company, use in Company's business, or cause Company to use, any trade secret of others.

4. Return of Materials

When Employee's employment with Company ends, for whatever reason, Employee will promptly deliver to Company all originals and copies of all documents, records, software programs, media and other materials containing any Confidential Information. Employee will also return to Company all equipment, files, software programs and other personal property belonging to Company.

5. Confidentiality Obligation Survives Employment

Employee's obligation to maintain the confidentiality and security of Confidential Information remains even after Employee's employment with Company ends and continues for so long as such Confidential Information remains a trade secret.

6. General Provisions

(a) Relationships: Nothing contained in this Agreement shall be deemed to make Employee a partner or joint venturer of Company for any purpose.

(b) Severability: If a court finds any provision of this Agreement invalid or unenforceable, the remainder of this Agreement shall be interpreted so as best to effect the intent of Company and Employee.

(c) Integration: This Agreement expresses the complete understanding of the parties with respect to the subject matter and supersedes all prior proposals, agreements, representations and understandings. This Agreement may not be amended except in a writing signed by both Company and Employee.

(d) Waiver: The failure to exercise any right provided in this Agreement shall not be a waiver of prior or subsequent rights.

(e) Injunctive Relief: Any misappropriation of any of the Confidential Information in violation of this Agreement may cause Company irreparable harm, the amount of which may be difficult to ascertain, and therefore Employee agrees that Company shall have the right to apply to a court of competent jurisdiction for an order enjoining any such further misappropriation and for such other relief as Company deems appropriate. This right is to be in addition to the remedies otherwise available to Company.

(f) Indemnity: Employee agrees to indemnify Company against any and all losses, damages, claims or expenses incurred or suffered by Company as a result of Employee's breach of this Agreement.

(g) Attorney Fees and Expenses: In a dispute arising out of or related to this Agreement, the prevailing party shall have the right to collect from the other party its reasonable attorney fees and costs and necessary expenditures.

(h) Governing Law. This Agreement shall be governed in accordance with the laws of the State of _____.

(i) Jurisdiction. Employee consents to the exclusive jurisdiction and venue of the federal and state courts located in _____ [*insert county and state in which parties agree to litigate*] in any action arising out of or relating to this Agreement. Employee waives any other venue to which Employee might be entitled by domicile or otherwise.

(j) Successors & Assigns. This Agreement shall bind each party's heirs, successors and assigns. Company may assign this Agreement to any party at any time. Employee shall not assign any of his or her rights or obligations under this Agreement without Company's prior written consent. Any assignment or transfer in violation of this section shall be void.

7. Signatures

Employee has carefully read all of this Agreement and agrees that all of the restrictions set forth are fair and reasonably required to protect Company's interests. Employee has received a copy of this Agreement as signed by the parties.

Employee:

_____

(Signature)

_____

(Typed or Printed Name)

Date:_____

Company:

_____

(Signature)

_____

(Typed or Printed Name)

Date: _____

Nondisclosure Agreement for Business Negotiations

This agreement between _____ (the "Disclosing Party") and
_____ (the "Receiving Party") is effective _____.
It is entered into to prevent the unauthorized disclosure of Confidential Information (as
defined below) of Disclosing Party which may be disclosed to Receiving Party for the purpose
of pursuing or establishing a business relationship or negotiating a contract between the
parties. Accordingly, the parties agree as follows:

1. Confidential Information

[Alternative 1]
The following information constitutes confidential proprietary trade secret information
("Confidential Information") belonging to Disclosing Party: _____.

[Alternative 2]
Disclosing Party's confidential proprietary trade secret information ("Confidential
Information") consists of information and materials that are valuable and not generally known
by Disclosing Party's competitors. Confidential Information includes:

(a) Any and all information concerning Disclosing Party's current, future or proposed
products, including, but not limited to, formulas, designs, devices, computer code, drawings,
specifications, notebook entries, technical notes and graphs, computer printouts, technical
memoranda and correspondence, product development agreements and related agreements.

(b) Information and materials relating to Disclosing Party's purchasing, accounting and
marketing, including, but not limited to, marketing plans, sales data, business methods,
unpublished promotional material, cost and pricing information and customer lists.

(c) Information of the type described above which Disclosing Party obtained from another
party and which Disclosing Party treats as confidential, whether or not owned or developed
by Disclosing Party.

(d) Other: _____.

2. Nondisclosure

Receiving Party will treat Confidential Information with the same degree of care and
safeguards that it takes with its own Confidential Information, but in no event less than a
reasonable degree of care. Without Disclosing Party's prior written consent, Receiving Party
will not:

(a) disclose Confidential Information to any third party;

(b) make or permit to be made copies or other reproductions of Confidential Information; or

(c) make any commercial use of Confidential Information.

Receiving Party will carefully restrict access to Confidential Information to those of its officers, directors and employees who are subject to nondisclosure restrictions at least as protective as those set forth in this Agreement and who clearly need such access to participate on Receiving Party's behalf in the analysis and negotiation of a business relationship or any contract or agreement with Disclosing Party.

Receiving Party will advise each officer, director or employee to whom it provides access to any Confidential Information that they are prohibited from using it or disclosing it to others without Disclosing Party's prior written consent.

[*Optional*]
In addition, without prior written consent of Disclosing Party, Receiving Party shall not disclose to any person either the fact that discussions or negotiations are taking place concerning a possible transaction or the status of such discussions or negotiations.

3. Return of Materials

Upon Disclosing Party's request, Receiving Party shall within 30 days return all original materials provided by Disclosing Party and any copies, notes or other documents in Receiving Party's possession pertaining to Confidential Information.

4. Exclusions

This agreement does not apply to any information that:

(a) was in Receiving Party's possession or was known to Receiving Party, without an obligation to keep it confidential, before such information was disclosed to Receiving Party by Disclosing Party;

(b) is or becomes public knowledge through a source other than Receiving Party and through no fault of Receiving Party;

(c) is or becomes lawfully available to Receiving Party from a source other than Disclosing Party; or

(d) is disclosed by Receiving Party with Disclosing Party's prior written approval.

5. Term

[Alternative 1]
This Agreement and Receiving Party's duty to hold Confidential Information in confidence shall remain in effect until Confidential Information is no longer a trade secret or until Disclosing Party sends Receiving Party written notice releasing Receiving Party from this Agreement, whichever occurs first.

[Alternative 2]
This Agreement and Receiving Party's duty to hold Confidential Information in confidence shall remain in effect until _____ or until whichever of the following occurs first:

(a) Disclosing Party sends Receiving Party written notice releasing it from this Agreement, or

(b) Confidential Information disclosed under this Agreement ceases to be a trade secret.

6. No Rights Granted

This Agreement does not constitute a grant or an intention or commitment to grant any right, title or interest in Confidential Information to Receiving Party.

7. Warranty

Disclosing Party warrants that it has the right to make the disclosures under this Agreement.

8. General Provisions

(a) Relationships: Nothing contained in this Agreement shall be deemed to constitute either party a partner, joint venturer or employee of the other party for any purpose.

(b) Severability: If a court finds any provision of this Agreement invalid or unenforceable, the remainder of this Agreement shall be interpreted so as best to effect the intent of the parties.

(c) Integration: This Agreement expresses the complete understanding of the parties with respect to the subject matter and supersedes all prior proposals, agreements, representations and understandings. This Agreement may not be amended except in a writing signed by both parties.

(d) Waiver: The failure to exercise any right provided in this Agreement shall not be a waiver of prior or subsequent rights.

(e) Injunctive Relief: Any misappropriation of Confidential Information in violation of this Agreement may cause Disclosing Party irreparable harm, the amount of which may be difficult to ascertain, and therefore Receiving Party agrees that Disclosing Party shall have the right to apply to a court of competent jurisdiction for an order enjoining any such further misappropriation and for such other relief as Disclosing Party deems appropriate. This right of Disclosing Party is to be in addition to the remedies otherwise available to Disclosing Party.

(f) Indemnity: Receiving Party agrees to indemnify Disclosing Party against any and all losses, damages, claims or expenses incurred or suffered by Disclosing Party as a result of Receiving Party's breach of this Agreement.

(g) Attorney Fees and Expenses: In a dispute arising out of or related to this Agreement, the prevailing party shall have the right to collect from the other party its reasonable attorney fees and costs and necessary expenditures.

(h) Governing Law: This Agreement shall be governed in accordance with the laws of the State of _____.

(i) Jurisdiction: The parties consent to the exclusive jurisdiction and venue of the federal and state courts located in _____ [insert county and state in which parties agree to litigate] in any action arising out of or relating to this Agreement. The parties waive any other venue to which either party might be entitled by domicile or otherwise.

(j) Successors & Assigns:

[Alternative 1]
This Agreement shall bind each party's heirs, successors and assigns. Receiving Party may not assign or transfer its rights or obligations under this Agreement without the prior written consent of Disclosing Party. Any assignment or transfer in violation of this section shall be void.

[Alternative 2 (Consent Not Unreasonably Withheld)]
This Agreement shall bind each party's heirs, successors and assigns. Receiving Party may not assign or transfer its rights or obligations under this Agreement without the prior written consent of Disclosing Party. Such consent shall not be unreasonably withheld. Any assignment or transfer in violation of this section shall be void.

[Alternative 3 (Consent not needed for affiliates or new owners)]
This Agreement shall bind each party's heirs, successors and assigns. Receiving Party may

not assign or transfer its rights or obligations under this Agreement without the prior written consent of Disclosing Party. However, no consent is required for an assignment or transfer that occurs: (a) to an entity in which Receiving Party owns more than fifty percent of the assets; or (b) as part of a transfer of all or substantially all of the assets of Receiving Party to any party. Any assignment or transfer in violation of this section shall be void.

Disclosing Party:

_____

(Signature)

_____

 (Typed or Printed Name)

Title: _____

Date: _____

Receiving Party:

_____

(Signature)

_____

(Typed or Printed Name)

Title: _____

Date: _____

Visitor Nondisclosure Agreement

Visitor's Name (*Print*): _____

Affiliation: _____

Place Visited: _____

Date(s) Visited: _____

1. I may be given access to confidential information belonging to
_____ (the "Company") through my relationship with Company or as
a result of my access to Company's premises.

2. I understand and acknowledge that Company's trade secrets consist of information and
materials that are valuable and not generally known by Company's competitors, including:

(a) Any and all information concerning Company's current, future or proposed products,
including, but not limited to, computer code, drawings, specifications, notebook entries,
technical notes and graphs, computer printouts, technical memoranda and correspondence,
product development agreements and related agreements.

(b) Information and materials relating to Company's purchasing, accounting and marketing;
including, but not limited to, marketing plans, sales data, unpublished promotional material,
cost and pricing information and customer lists.

(c) Information of the type described above which Company obtained from another party
and which Company treats as confidential, whether or not owned or developed by
Company.

(d) Other: _____.

3. In consideration of being admitted to Company's facilities, I will hold in the strictest
confidence any trade secrets or confidential information that is disclosed to me. I will not
remove any document, equipment or other materials from the premises without Company's
written permission. I will not photograph or otherwise record any information to which I may
have access during my visit.

4. This Agreement is binding on me, my heirs, executors, administrators and assigns and
inures to the benefit of Company, its successors and assigns.

5. This Agreement constitutes the entire understanding between Company and me with respect to its subject matter. It supersedes all earlier representations and understandings, whether oral or written.

Visitor:

_____

(Signature)

_____

(Typed or Printed Name)

Date: _____

Interview Nondisclosure Agreement

_____ ("Company") and _____ ("Applicant") agree as follows:

1. Company is interviewing Applicant for the position of _____ and to work on the following projects: _____.

2. Company's trade secrets may be disclosed during the interview process or as a result of Applicant's access to Company's premises.

3. Company's trade secrets consist of information and materials that are valuable and not generally known by Company's competitors, including:

(a) Any and all information concerning Company's current, future or proposed products, including, but not limited to, computer code, drawings, specifications, notebook entries, technical notes and graphs, computer printouts, technical memoranda and correspondence, product development agreements and related agreements.

(b) Information and materials relating to Company's purchasing, accounting and marketing; including, but not limited to, marketing plans, sales data, unpublished promotional material, cost and pricing information and customer lists.

(c) Information of the type described above which Company obtained from another party and which Company treats as confidential, whether or not owned or developed by Company.

(d) Other: _____.

4. At all times, Applicant will keep confidential and will not make use of or disclose to any third party any of Company's trade secrets.

5. Applicant will not use, disclose to Company, or cause Company to use any trade secret or confidential information of any other person or entity.

Company:

_____

(Signature)

_____

(Typed or Printed Name)

Title: _____

Date: _____

Applicant:

_____

(Signature)

_____

(Typed or Printed Name)

Date: _____

Software Beta Tester Nondisclosure Agreement

This is an agreement, effective _____, between _____ ("Company") and _____ ("Tester"), in which Tester agrees to test a software program known as _____ (the "Software") and keep Company aware of the test results.

1. Company's Obligations

Company shall provide Tester with a copy of Software and any necessary documentation and instruct Tester on how to use it and what test data is desired by Company. Upon satisfactory completion of the testing,

[*Choose One*]

❑ Company shall furnish Tester with one free copy of the production version of Software, contingent upon Company's decision to proceed with production of Software.

❑ _____.

Tester shall be entitled to the same benefits to which regular purchasers of Software will be entitled.

2. Tester's Obligations

Tester shall test Software under normally expected operating conditions in Tester's environment during the test period. Tester shall gather and report test data as agreed upon with Company. Tester shall allow Company access to Software during normal working hours for inspection, modifications and maintenance.

3. Software a Trade Secret

Software is proprietary to, and a valuable trade secret of, Company. It is entrusted to Tester only for the purpose set forth in this Agreement. Tester shall maintain Software in the strictest confidence. Tester will not, without Company's prior written consent:

(a) disclose any information about Software, its design and performance specifications, its code, and the existence of the beta test and its results to anyone other than Tester's employees who are performing the testing and who shall be subject to nondisclosure restrictions at least as protective as those set forth in this Agreement;

(b) copy any portion of Software or documentation, except to the extent necessary to perform beta testing; or

(c) reverse engineer, decompile or disassemble Software or any portion of it.

4. Security Precautions

Tester shall take reasonable security precautions to prevent Software from being seen by unauthorized individuals whether stored on Tester's hard drive or on physical copies such as CD-ROMS, diskettes or other media. Tester shall lock all copies of Software and associated documentation in a desk or file cabinet when not in use.

5. Term of Agreement

The test period shall last from _____, until _____. This Agreement shall terminate at the end of the test period or when Company asks Tester to return Software, whichever occurs first. The restrictions and obligations contained in Clauses 4, 7, 8, 9 and 10 shall survive the expiration, termination or cancellation of this Agreement, and shall continue to bind Tester, its successors, heirs and assigns.

6. Return of Software and Materials

Upon the conclusion of the testing period or at Company's request, Tester shall within 10 days return the original and all copies of Software and all related materials to Company and delete all portions of Software from computer memory.

7. Disclaimer of Warranty

Software is a test product and its accuracy and reliability are not guaranteed. Tester shall not rely exclusively on Software for any reason. Tester waives any and all claims Tester may have against Company arising out of the performance or nonperformance of Software.

SOFTWARE IS PROVIDED AS IS, AND COMPANY DISCLAIMS ANY AND ALL REPRESENTATIONS OR WARRANTIES OF ANY KIND, WHETHER EXPRESS OR IMPLIED, WITH RESPECT TO IT, INCLUDING ANY IMPLIED WARRANTIES OF MERCHANTABILITY OR FITNESS FOR A PARTICULAR PURPOSE.

8. Limitation of Liability

Company shall not be responsible for any loss or damage to Tester or any third parties caused by Software. COMPANY SHALL NOT BE LIABLE FOR ANY DIRECT, INDIRECT, SPECIAL, INCIDENTAL OR CONSEQUENTIAL DAMAGE, WHETHER BASED ON CONTRACT OR TORT OR ANY OTHER LEGAL THEORY, ARISING OUT OF ANY USE OF SOFTWARE OR ANY PERFORMANCE OF THIS AGREEMENT.

9. No Rights Granted

This Agreement does not constitute a grant or an intention or commitment to grant any right, title or interest in Software or Company's trade secrets to Tester. Tester may not sell or transfer any portion of Software to any third party or use Software in any manner to produce, market or support its own products. Tester shall not identify Software as coming from any source other than Company.

10. No Assignments

This Agreement is personal to Tester. Tester shall not assign or otherwise transfer any rights or obligations under this Agreement.

11. General Provisions

(a) Relationships: Nothing contained in this Agreement shall be deemed to constitute either party a partner, joint venturer or employee of the other party for any purpose.

(b) Severability: If a court finds any provision of this Agreement invalid or unenforceable, the remainder of this Agreement shall be interpreted so as best to effect the intent of the parties.

(c) Integration: This Agreement expresses the complete understanding of the parties with respect to the subject matter and supersedes all prior proposals, agreements, representations and understandings. This Agreement may not be amended except in a writing signed by both parties.

(d) Waiver: The failure to exercise any right provided in this Agreement shall not be a waiver of prior or subsequent rights.

(e) Attorney Fees and Expenses: In a dispute arising out of or related to this Agreement, the prevailing party shall have the right to collect from the other party its reasonable attorney fees and costs and necessary expenditures.

(f) Governing Law: This Agreement shall be governed in accordance with the laws of the State of _____.

(g) Jurisdiction: The parties consent to the exclusive jurisdiction and venue of the federal and state courts located in _____ [insert county and state in which parties agree to litigate] in any action arising out of or relating to this Agreement. The parties waive any other venue to which either party might be entitled by domicile or otherwise.

Company:

_____

(Signature)

_____

(Typed or Printed Name)

Title: _____

Date: _____

Tester:

_____

(Signature)

_____

(Typed or Printed Name)

Date: _____

Nondisclosure Agreement for Licensee

This agreement, effective _____ between _____ ("Company") and _____ ("Customer"), is entered into to authorize Customer to receive from Company and evaluate certain proprietary computer software and documentation known as _____, ("Software").

1. Nonexclusive License

Company grants Customer a nonexclusive license to install Software on its computer system and use Software for a period of _____ days from the date of delivery. Customer shall use Software only for the purpose of evaluating its performance and not for a productive purpose. Customer shall acquire no other intellectual property rights under this Agreement.

2. Software a Trade Secret

Software is proprietary to, and a valuable trade secret of, Company.

3. Nondisclosure

In consideration of Company's disclosure of Software to Customer, Customer will treat Software with the same degree of care and safeguards that it takes with its own trade secrets, but in no event less than a reasonable degree of care. Customer will not, without Company's prior written consent:

(a) reverse engineer, decompile or disassemble Software or any portion of it;

(b) copy any portion of Software;

(c) download Software in a retrieval system or computer system of any kind except as authorized by this Agreement; or

(d) disclose any portion of Software to any third party.

Customer will limit use of Software to those employees, agents and consultants of Customer who are performing the evaluation for Customer. Customer must advise such people that Software is Company's trade secret and they must be under an express written obligation to maintain its confidentiality.

The restrictions and obligations contained in this clause will remain in effect until Software no longer constitutes a trade secret or until Company sends Customer written notice releasing it from this Agreement, whichever occurs first.

4. Return of Software and Materials

Customer shall promptly return Software and all related materials to Company and delete all copies and portions of Software from computer memory upon the termination of this Agreement, Company's request, or the Customer's decision not to purchase or license Software, whichever occurs first.

5. Limitation of Liability

Company shall not be responsible for any loss or damage to Customer or any third parties caused by Customer's use of Software.

COMPANY SHALL NOT BE LIABLE FOR ANY DIRECT, INDIRECT, SPECIAL, INCIDENTAL OR CONSEQUENTIAL DAMAGES, WHETHER BASED ON CONTRACT OR TORT OR ANY OTHER LEGAL THEORY, ARISING OUT OF ANY USE OF SOFTWARE OR ANY PERFORMANCE OF THIS AGREEMENT.

6. General Provisions

(a) Relationships: Nothing contained in this Agreement shall be deemed to constitute either party a partner, joint venturer or employee of the other party for any purpose.

(b) Severability: If a court finds any provision of this Agreement invalid or unenforceable, the remainder of this Agreement shall be interpreted so as best to effect the intent of the parties.

(c) Integration: This Agreement expresses the complete understanding of the parties with respect to the subject matter and supersedes all prior proposals, agreements, representations and understandings. This Agreement may not be amended except in a writing signed by both parties.

(d) Waiver: The failure to exercise any right provided in this Agreement shall not be a waiver of prior or subsequent rights.

(e) Injunctive Relief: Customer acknowledges that any misappropriation of any of the Confidential Information in violation of this Agreement may cause Company irreparable harm, the amount of which may be difficult to ascertain, and therefore agrees that Company shall have the right to apply to a court of competent jurisdiction for an order enjoining any such further misappropriation and for such other relief as Company deems appropriate. This right of Company is to be in addition to the remedies otherwise available to Company.

(f) Indemnity: Customer agrees to indemnify Company against any and all losses, damages, claims or expenses incurred or suffered by Company as a result of the Customer's breach of this Agreement.

(g) Attorney Fees and Expenses: In a dispute arising out of or related to this Agreement, the prevailing party shall have the right to collect from the other party its reasonable attorney fees and costs and necessary expenditures.

(h) Governing Law: This Agreement shall be governed in accordance with the laws of the State of _____.

(i) Jurisdiction: The parties consent to the exclusive jurisdiction and venue of the federal and state courts located in_____[insert county and state in which parties agree to litigate] in any action arising out of or relating to this Agreement. The parties waive any other venue to which either party might be entitled by domicile or otherwise.

(j) Successors and Assigns: This Agreement shall bind each party's heirs, successors and assigns. Customer may not assign or transfer its rights or obligations under this Agreement without the prior written consent of Company. Any assignment or transfer in violation of this section shall be void.

Company:

_____
(Signature)

_____
(Typed or Printed Name)

Title: _____

Date: _____

Customer:

_____
(Signature)

_____
(Typed or Printed Name)

Date: _____

Student Nondisclosure Agreement

In consideration of being given access to information that will be valuable for my research or study in the area of: _____[describe] by _____ [full name of university or college] ("Disclosing Party"), I agree as follows:

1. Trade Secrets

I understand that during the course of my study and/or research there may be disclosed to me or I may gain access to trade secrets and other proprietary or confidential information of Disclosing Party. This includes, but is not limited to:

(a) technical information concerning Disclosing Party's research projects, technical memoranda and correspondence, formulas, designs, devices, diagrams, software code, test results, processes, inventions; and

(b) Disclosing Party's business information, including cost information, accounting and unpublished financial information, business plans, customer lists and customer information, purchasing techniques, supplier lists and supplier information and marketing, production or merchandising systems or plans;

2. Nondisclosure of Trade Secrets

I will keep Disclosing Party's trade secrets, whether or not prepared or developed by me, in the strictest confidence. I will not disclose such secrets to anyone outside Disclosing Party without Disclosing Party's prior written consent. Nor will I make use of any Disclosing Party trade secrets for my own purposes or the benefit of anyone other than Disclosing Party without Disclosing Party's prior written consent.

However, I have no obligation to treat as confidential any information which:

(a) was in my possession or known to me, without an obligation to keep it confidential, before such information was disclosed to me by Disclosing Party;

(b) is or becomes public knowledge through a source other than me and through no fault of Employee; or

(c) is or becomes lawfully available to me from a source other than Disclosing Party.

3. Return of Materials

When my research or study with Disclosing Party ends, for whatever reason, I will promptly deliver to Disclosing Party all originals and copies of all documents, records, software programs, media and other materials containing any of Disclosing Party's trade secrets. I will also return to Disclosing Party all equipment, files, software programs and other personal property belonging to Disclosing Party.

4. Review of Papers or Publications

For a period of _____ years, I will submit to _____ [Name] a full and complete draft of any papers, reports or proposed publications that include any information derived from my research or study with Disclosing Party for its review. I shall disguise or excise from this material any data that Disclosing Party identifies as too sensitive for disclosure.

5. Duration of Confidentiality Obligation

My obligation to maintain the confidentiality and security of Disclosing Party's trade secrets continues for so long as such material remains a trade secret.

6. General Provisions

(a) Relationships: Nothing contained in this Agreement shall be deemed to make me a partner, joint venturer or employee of Disclosing Party for any purpose.

(b) Severability: If a court finds any provision of this Agreement invalid or unenforceable, the remainder of this Agreement shall be interpreted so as best to effect the intent of Disclosing Party and myself.

(c) Integration: This Agreement expresses the complete understanding of the parties with respect to the subject matter and supersedes all prior proposals, agreements, representations and understandings. This Agreement may not be amended except in a writing signed by both Disclosing Party and myself.

(d) Waiver: The failure to exercise any right provided in this Agreement shall not be a waiver of prior or subsequent rights.

(e) Injunctive Relief: I acknowledge that any misappropriation of any of the Confidential Information in violation of this Agreement may cause Disclosing Party irreparable harm, the amount of which may be difficult to ascertain, and therefore agree that Disclosing Party shall have the right to apply to a court of competent jurisdiction for an order enjoining any such further misappropriation and for such other relief as Disclosing Party deems appropriate. This right is to be in addition to the remedies otherwise available to Disclosing Party.

(f) Indemnity: I agree to indemnify Disclosing Party against any and all losses, damages, claims or expenses incurred or suffered by Disclosing Party as a result of my breach of this Agreement.

(g) Attorney Fees and Expenses: In a dispute arising out of or related to this Agreement, the prevailing party shall have the right to collect from the other party its reasonable attorney fees and costs and necessary expenditures.

(h) Governing Law. This Agreement shall be governed in accordance with the laws of the State of _____.

(i) Jurisdiction. I consent to the exclusive jurisdiction and venue of the federal and state courts located in_____[*insert county and state in which parties agree to litigate*] in any action arising out of or relating to this Agreement. I waive any other venue to which I might be entitled by domicile or otherwise.

(j) Successors & Assigns. This Agreement shall bind each party's heirs, successors and assigns. Disclosing Party may assign this Agreement to any party at any time. I shall not assign any of its rights or obligations under this Agreement without Disclosing Party's prior written consent. Any assignment or transfer in violation of this section shall be void.

7. Signature

I have carefully read and considered all clauses of this Agreement and agree that all of the restrictions set forth are fair and reasonably required to protect Disclosing Party's interests. I have received a copy of this Agreement as signed by me.

Student:

_____

(Signature)

_____

(Typed or Printed Name)

Date: _____

Customer List/Mailing List Nondisclosure Agreement

For valuable consideration, the receipt and sufficiency of which is hereby acknowledged, _____[*Full name of company*] ("Disclosing Party") authorizes _____[*Full name of Receiving Party*] ("Receiving Party") to use the customer list/mailing list identified as _____ [*Provide name for list*] ("List") under the following terms and conditions:

1. List a Trade Secret

Receiving Party understands and acknowledges that List is a valuable trade secret belonging to Disclosing Party.

2. Purpose of Disclosure

Receiving Party shall use the List only for the following purposes: _____ [*Describe—for example "to distribute Receiving Party's advertising or promotional material. "*]

3. Receiving Party's Obligations

Receiving Party shall hold and maintain the List in the strictest confidence. Receiving Party shall carefully restrict access to the List only to persons bound by this Agreement and only on a need-to-know basis. Receiving Party shall not, without Disclosing Party's prior written approval, publish, copy, or otherwise disclose the List to others, or permit its use by others for their benefit or to Disclosing Party's detriment.

4. Term

[*Alternative 1*]
This Agreement and Receiving Party's duty to hold the List in confidence shall remain in effect until the List is no longer a trade secret or until Disclosing Party sends Receiving Party written notice releasing Receiving Party from this Agreement, whichever occurs first.

[*Alternative 2*]
This Agreement and Receiving Party's duty to hold the List in confidence shall remain in effect until _____ or until whichever of the following occurs first:

(a) Disclosing Party sends Receiving Party written notice releasing Receiving Party from this Agreement, or

(b) The List is no longer a trade secret.

5. No Rights Granted

Receiving Party understands and agrees that this Agreement does not constitute a grant or an intention or commitment to grant any right, title or interest in the List or any other of Disclosing Party's trade secrets to Receiving Party.

6. Warranty

Disclosing Party warrants that it has the right to make the disclosures under this Agreement.

7. General Provisions

(a) Relationships: Nothing contained in this Agreement shall be deemed to constitute either party a partner, joint venturer or employee of the other party for any purpose.

(b) Severability: If a court finds any provision of this Agreement invalid or unenforceable, the remainder of this Agreement shall be interpreted so as best to effect the intent of the parties.

(c) Integration: This Agreement expresses the complete understanding of the parties with respect to the subject matter and supersedes all prior proposals, agreements, representations and understandings. This Agreement may not be amended except in a writing signed by both parties.

(d) Waiver: The failure to exercise any right provided in this Agreement shall not be a waiver of prior or subsequent rights.

(e) Injunctive Relief: Receiving Party acknowledges that any misappropriation of any of the Confidential Information in violation of this Agreement may cause Disclosing Party irreparable harm, the amount of which may be difficult to ascertain, and therefore agrees that Disclosing Party shall have the right to apply to a court of competent jurisdiction for an order enjoining any such further misappropriation and for such other relief as Disclosing Party deems appropriate. This right of Disclosing Party is to be in addition to the remedies otherwise available to Disclosing Party.

(f) Indemnity: Receiving Party agrees to indemnify Disclosing Party against any and all losses, damages, claims or expenses incurred or suffered by Disclosing Party as a result of Receiving Party's breach of this Agreement.

(g) Attorney Fees and Expenses: In a dispute arising out of or related to this Agreement, the prevailing party shall have the right to collect from the other party its reasonable attorney fees and costs and necessary expenditures.

(h) Governing Law: This Agreement shall be governed in accordance with the laws of the State of _____.

(i) Jurisdiction: The parties consent to the exclusive jurisdiction and venue of the federal and state courts located in _____*[insert county and state in which parties agree to litigate]* in any action arising out of or relating to this Agreement. The parties waive any other venue to which either party might be entitled by domicile or otherwise.

(j) Successors & Assigns: This Agreement shall bind each party's heirs, successors and assigns. Receiving Party may not assign or transfer its rights or obligations under this Agreement without the prior written consent of Disclosing Party. Any assignment or transfer in violation of this section shall be void.

Disclosing Party:

_____

(Signature)

_____

(Typed or Printed Name)

Date: _____

Receiving Party:

_____

(Signature)

_____

(Typed or Printed Name)

Title: _____

Date: _____

Sample Employer Ownership Provisions

Assignment of Intellectual Property. Employee agrees that any trade secret, process, system, discovery, improvement, copyrightable work of authorship or patentable creation (Innovations) conceived, originated, discovered or developed in whole or in part by Employee: (1) as a result of any work performed by Employee with Company's equipment, supplies, facilities, trade secret information, or other Company resources; or (2) on Company's time shall be the sole and exclusive property of Company, provided that the Innovation relates to Company's business or anticipated research. Employee acknowledges that any copyrightable works created within the course of employment are works made for hire as defined under copyright law. Employee agrees to sign and deliver to Company (either during or subsequent to Employee's employment) such documents as Company considers desirable to evidence Employee's assignment of rights or Company's ownership of such Innovations. All documentation or records reflecting any Innovations belong exclusively to Company and shall be delivered to Company by Employee when Employee is no longer employed by Company.

Power of Attorney. In the event Company is unable to secure Employee's signature on any document necessary to apply for, prosecute, obtain or enforce any legal right or protection relating to any Innovation or copyrightable work referred to above, Employee irrevocably designates and appoints Company (and each of its duly authorized officers and agents) as Employee's agent and attorney-in-fact, to act for and in Employee's behalf and to execute and file any such document and to do all other lawfully permitted acts to further the prosecution, issuance and enforcement of patents, copyrights or other rights.

Duty to Disclose. Employee agrees to promptly disclose in writing to Company all discoveries, developments, designs, code, ideas, innovations, improvements, trade secrets, formulas, processes, techniques, know-how, and data (whether or not patentable or registrable under copyright or similar statutes) made, written, conceived, reduced to practice or learned by Employee (either alone or jointly with others) that are related to or useful in Company's business, or that result from tasks assigned to Employee by Company, or from the use of facilities owned, leased or otherwise acquired by Company.

Independent Contractor Agreement

This Agreement (the "Agreement") is made between _____
("Company"), and _____ ("Contractor").

Services. Contractor agrees to perform the following services:

_____

The services shall be completed by the following date: _____

During the process, Contractor shall keep the Company informed of work in progress.

Payment. Company agrees to pay Contractor as follows:

$_____ for the services and acquisition of the rights provided below.

Assignment, Works Made for Hire. Contractor assigns to Company any trade secret, process, system, trademarks or patentable creation (Innovations) created by or discovered or developed in whole or in part by Contractor as a result of any work performed by Contractor under this Agreement. Such Innovations shall be the sole and exclusive property of Company. Any works of authorship ("Works") commissioned pursuant to this Agreement shall be considered as works made for hire as that term is defined under U.S. copyright law. To the extent that any Works do not qualify as a work made for hire, Contractor hereby assigns and transfers to Company all rights in such Works.

Contractor agrees to sign and deliver to Company (either during or subsequent to commencing work) such documents as Company considers desirable to evidence: (1) the assignment to Company of all rights of Contractor, if any, in any such Innovation or Work, and (2) Company's ownership of such Innovations and Works.

Power of Attorney. In the event Company is unable to secure Contractor's signature on any document necessary to apply for, prosecute, obtain or enforce any legal right or protection relating to any Innovation or Works referred to above, Contractor irrevocably designates and appoints Company (and each of its duly authorized officers and agents) as his agent and attorney-in-fact, to act for and in his behalf and to execute and file any such document and to do all other lawfully permitted acts to further the prosecution, issuance and enforcement of patents, copyrights or other rights.

Contractor Warranties. Contractor warrants that any Innovations or Works created by Contractor shall not infringe any intellectual property rights or violate any laws.

Confidential Information. For purposes of this Agreement, "Confidential Information" shall include all information or material that has or could have commercial value or other utility in the business in which Company is engaged. If Confidential Information is in written form, Company shall label or stamp the materials with the word "Confidential" or some similar warning. If Confidential Information is transmitted orally, Company shall promptly provide a writing indicating that such oral communication constituted Confidential Information.

Contractor's obligations not to disclose Confidential Information do not extend to information that is: (a) publicly known at the time of disclosure under this Agreement or subsequently becomes publicly known through no fault of Contractor; (b) discovered or created by Contractor prior to disclosure by Company; (c) otherwise learned by Contractor through legitimate means other than from Company or Company's representatives; or (d) is disclosed by Contractor with Company's prior written approval.

Contractor shall hold and maintain the Confidential Information of Company in strictest confidence for the sole and exclusive benefit of Company. Contractor shall carefully restrict access to Confidential Information to employees, contractors and third parties as is reasonably required and only to persons subject to nondisclosure restrictions at least as protective as those set forth in this Agreement. Contractor shall not, without prior written approval of Company, use for Contractor's own benefit, publish, copy, or otherwise disclose to others, or permit the use by others for their benefit or to the detriment of Company, any Confidential Information. Contractor shall return to Company any and all records, notes, and other written, printed, or tangible materials in its possession pertaining to Confidential Information immediately if Company requests it in writing.

The nondisclosure and confidentiality provisions of this Agreement shall survive the termination of any relationship between Company and Contractor except that this Agreement and Contractor's duty to hold Company's Confidential Information in confidence shall remain in effect until the Confidential Information no longer qualifies as a trade secret or until Company sends Contractor written notice releasing Contractor from this Agreement, whichever occurs first.

Relationships. Nothing contained in this Agreement shall be deemed to constitute either party a partner, joint venturer or employee of the other party for any purpose.

Severability. If a court finds any provision of this Agreement invalid or unenforceable, the remainder of this Agreement shall be interpreted so as best to effect the intent of the parties.

Integration. This Agreement expresses the complete understanding of the parties with respect to the subject matter and supersedes all prior proposals, agreements, representations and understandings. This Agreement may not be amended except in a writing signed by both parties.

Waiver. The failure to exercise any right provided in this Agreement shall not be a waiver of prior or subsequent rights.

This Agreement and each party's obligations shall be binding on the representatives, assigns and successors of such party. Each party has signed this Agreement through its authorized representative.

Contractor:

_____

(Signature)

_____

(Typed or Printed Name)

Title: _____

Date: _____

Contractor:

_____

(Signature)

_____

(Typed or Printed Name)

Title: _____

Date: _____

Assignment of Intellectual Property Rights

_____ is the owner of all proprietary and intellectual property rights, including trade secrets, copyrights and patents, in the concepts and technologies known as _____ and more specifically described in Attachment A [*attach a description of the confidential information to the Assignment and label it "Attachment A"*] to this Assignment (and referred to collectively as the "Properties") and the right to registrations to the Properties; and _____ ("Assignee") desires to acquire the ownership of all proprietary rights, including, but not limited to the copyrights, trade secrets, trademarks and associated goodwill and patent rights in the Properties and the registrations to the Properties;

Therefore, for valuable consideration, the receipt of which is acknowledged, Assignor assigns to Assignee ___% [*insert percentage of interest that is being assigned—it can be less than 100%*] of all rights, title and interest in the Properties, including:

(1) all copyrights, trade secrets, trademarks and associated good will and all patents which may be granted on the Properties;

(2) all applications for patents (including divisions, continuations in whole or part or substitute applications) in the United States or any foreign countries whose duty it is to issue such patents;

(3) any reissues and extensions of such patents; and

(4) all priority rights under the International Convention for the Protection of Industrial Property for every member country.

Assignor warrants that: (1) Assignor is the legal owner of all rights, title and interest in the Properties; (2) that such rights have not been previously licensed, pledged, assigned, or encumbered; and (3) that this assignment does not infringe on the rights of any person. Assignor agrees to cooperate with Assignee and to execute and deliver all papers, instruments and assignments as may be necessary to vest all right, title and interest in and to the intellectual property rights to the Properties in Assignor. Assignor further agrees to testify in any legal proceeding, sign all lawful papers and applications and make all rightful oaths and generally do everything possible to aid Assignee to obtain and enforce proper protection for the Properties in all countries.

Date: _____ Assignor _____

[*to be completed by notary public*]
[*Add Notarization*]

Noncompete Provision
(Can Be Added to Nondisclosure Agreement)

Employee agrees that in order to protect the Confidential Information while Employee is employed by Company, and for a period of_____ thereafter, Employee shall not:

(a) plan for, acquire any financial interest in or perform services for (as an employee, consultant, officer, director, independent contractor, principal, agent or otherwise) any business that would require Employee to use or disclose any Confidential Information; or

(b) perform services (as an employee, consultant, officer, director, independent contractor, principal, agent or otherwise) that are similar to Employee's current duties or responsibilities for any person or entity that, during the Term, engages in any business activity in which Company is then engaged or proposes to be engaged and that conducts its business in the following territory: _____.

Nonsolicitation Provision
(Can Be Added to Nondisclosure Agreement)

While Employee is employed by Company, and for a period of _____ thereafter, Employee shall not:

(a) employ, attempt to employ or solicit for employment by any other person or entity, any Company employees;

(b) encourage any consultant, independent contractor or any other person or entity to end their relationship or stop doing business with Company, or help any person or entity do so or attempt to do so;

(c) solicit or attempt to solicit or obtain business or trade from any of Company's current or prospective customers or clients or help any person or entity do so or attempt to do so; or

(d) obtain or attempt to obtain any Confidential Information for any purpose whatsoever except as required by Company to enable Employee to perform his or her job duties.

Employee Noncompetition & Nonsolicitation Agreement

This agreement (the "Agreement") is entered into by and between
_____ ("Company") and _____ ("Employee")

1. Consideration

[*Alternative 1*]
In consideration of the commencement of Employee's employment with Company and the compensation that will be paid, Employee and Company agree as follows:

[*Alternative 2*]
In consideration of Employee's continued employment with Company and also in consideration of:

[*Choose one*]
❏ the amount of $_____

❏ options to purchase _____ shares of Company's stock

❏ _____

the receipt and sufficiency of which is acknowledged, the parties agree as follows:

2. Company's Confidential Information

In the performance of Employee's job duties with Company, Employee will be exposed to Company's Confidential Information. "Confidential Information" means information or material that is commercially valuable to Company and not generally known in the industry. This includes, but is not limited to:

(a) technical information concerning Company's products and services, including product know-how, formulas, designs, devices, diagrams, software code, test results, processes, inventions, research projects and product development, technical memoranda and correspondence;

(b) information concerning Company's business, including cost information, profits, sales information, accounting and unpublished financial information, business plans, markets and marketing methods, customer lists and customer information, purchasing techniques, supplier lists and supplier information and advertising strategies;

(c) information concerning Company's employees, including salaries, strengths, weaknesses and skills;

(d) information submitted by Company's customers, suppliers, employees, consultants or co-venture partners with Company for study, evaluation or use; and

(e) any other information not generally known to the public which, if misused or disclosed, could reasonably be expected to adversely affect Company's business.

3. Nondisclosure of Confidential Information

Employee shall keep Confidential Information, whether or not prepared or developed by Employee, in the strictest confidence. Employee will not disclose such secrets to anyone outside Company without Company's prior written consent. Nor will Employee make use of any Confidential Information for Employee's own purposes or the benefit of anyone other than Company.

However, Employee shall have no obligation to treat as confidential any information which:

(a) was in Employee's possession or known to Employee, without an obligation to keep it confidential, before such information was disclosed to Employee by Company;

(b) is or becomes public knowledge through a source other than Employee and through no fault of Employee; or

(c) is or becomes lawfully available to Employee from a source other than Company.

4. Noncompetition.

To protect the Confidential Information while Employee is employed by Company, and for a period of _____ thereafter, Employee shall not:

(a) plan for, acquire any financial interest in or perform services for (as an employee, consultant, officer, director, independent contractor, principal, agent or otherwise) any business that would require Employee to use or disclose any Confidential Information; or

(b) perform services (as an employee, consultant, officer, director, independent contractor, principal, agent or otherwise) that are similar to Employee's current duties or responsibilities for any person or entity that, during the Term, engages in any business activity in which Company is then engaged or proposes to be engaged and that conducts its business in the following territory: _____.

5. Nonsolicitation.

While Employee is employed by Company, and for a period of _____ thereafter, Employee shall not:

(a) employ, attempt to employ or solicit for employment by any other person or entity, any Company employees;

(b) encourage any consultant, independent contractor or any other person or entity to end their relationship or stop doing business with Company, or help any person or entity do so or attempt to do so;

(c) solicit or attempt to solicit or obtain business or trade from any of Company's current or prospective customers or clients or help any person or entity do so or attempt to do so; or

(d) obtain or attempt to obtain any Confidential Information for any purpose whatsoever except as required by Company to enable Employee to perform his or her job duties.

6. Confidential Information of Others

Employee will not disclose to Company, use in Company's business, or cause Company to use, any information or material that is a trade secret of others.

7. Return of Materials

When Employee's employment with Company ends, for whatever reason, Employee will promptly deliver to Company all originals and copies of all documents, records, software programs, media and other materials containing any Confidential Information. Employee will also return to Company all equipment, files, software programs and other personal property belonging to Company.

8. Confidentiality Obligation Survives Employment

Employee's obligation to maintain the confidentiality and security of Company's Confidential Information remains with Employee even after Employee's employment with Company ends and continues for so long as the Confidential Information remains a trade secret.

9. Enforcement

In the event of a breach or threatened breach of this Agreement, money damages would be an inadequate remedy and extremely difficult to measure. Company shall be entitled to an injunction to restrain Employee from such breach or threatened breach. Nothing in this

Agreement shall be construed as preventing Company from pursuing any remedy at law or in equity for any breach or threatened breach.

10. General Provisions

(a) Relationships: Nothing contained in this Agreement shall be deemed to make Employee a partner or joint venturer of Company for any purpose.

(b) Severability: If a court finds any provision of this Agreement invalid or unenforceable, the remainder of this Agreement shall be interpreted so as best to effect the intent of the parties.

(c) Integration: This Agreement expresses the complete understanding of the parties with respect to the subject matter and supersedes all prior proposals, agreements, representations and understandings. This Agreement may not be amended except in a writing signed by both Company and Employee.

(d) Waiver: The failure to exercise any right provided in this Agreement shall not be a waiver of prior or subsequent rights.

(e) Indemnity: Employee shall indemnify Company against any and all losses, damages, claims or expenses incurred or suffered by Company as a result of Employee's breach of this Agreement.

(f) Attorney Fees and Expenses: In a dispute arising out of or related to this Agreement, the prevailing party shall have the right to collect from the other party its reasonable attorney fees and costs and necessary expenditures.

(g) Governing Law. This Agreement shall be governed in accordance with the laws of the State of _____.

(h) Jurisdiction. In any dispute arising out of or under this Agreement, jurisdiction and venue of the dispute shall be federal and state courts located in _____[insert county and state in which parties agree to litigate]. Employee waives any other venue to which Employee might be entitled by domicile or otherwise.

(i) Assignability: Employee may not assign or transfer rights or obligations pursuant to this Agreement without the prior written consent of Company. Any assignment or transfer in violation of this section shall be void.

(j) Successors: The rights and obligations under this Agreement shall survive the termination of Employee's service to Company in any capacity and shall inure to the benefit and shall be binding upon: (1) Employee's heirs and personal representatives, and (2) the successors and assigns of Company.

11. Signatures

Employee has carefully read and considered all clauses of this Agreement and agree that all of the restrictions set forth are fair and reasonably required to protect Company's interests. Employee has received a copy of this Agreement as signed by both parties.

Employee:

_____

(Signature)

_____

(Typed or Printed Name)

Date: _____

Company:

_____

(Signature)

_____

(Typed or Printed Name)

Date: _____

Evaluation Agreement

_____ ("Disclosing Party") and _____
("Evaluating Party") agree as follows:

1. The Submission. Disclosing Party wishes to have Evaluating Party examine and evaluate a submission tentatively known as "_____" and more specifically described in Attachment A to this Agreement (the "Submission") with an eye toward assisting in the exploitation of any products, services or other commercial exploitation derived from materials contained in the Submission.

2. Review and Evaluation. Evaluating Party wishes to review the Submission and consider whether, in its opinion, the Submission can be marketed to the parties' mutual benefit. The materials furnished by Disclosing Party shall be used by Evaluating Party solely to review or evaluate the Submission. After evaluating the Submission, Evaluating Party will either offer to enter into an agreement with Disclosing Party for exploitation of the idea or return the Submission to Disclosing Party and agree not to market or participate in the marketing or exploitation of any product or service described in or derived from the Submission.

3. Nonexclusivity. Disclosing Party retains the right to submit the Submission to others while it is being evaluated by Evaluating Party.

4. Confidentiality. The materials submitted by Disclosing Party describing the Submission, constitute valuable confidential information of Disclosing Party. The loss or outside disclosure of these materials or the information contained within them will harm Disclosing Party economically. Evaluating Party agrees to hold the Submission confidential and will not disclose it to any person other than its evaluators and other members of its staff who have reason to view the Submission.

Evaluating Party shall exercise a high degree of care to safeguard these materials and the information they contain from access or disclosure to all unauthorized persons. All applicable rights to the Submission remain vested in Disclosing Party. The foregoing provisions apply with equal force to any additional or supplemental submissions and other materials submitted or to be submitted by Disclosing Party to Evaluating Party with respect to the same subject matter of the Submission.

5. Relationships. Nothing contained in this Agreement shall be deemed to constitute either party a partner, joint venturer or employee of the other party for any purpose.

6. Severability. If a court finds any provision of this Agreement invalid or unenforceable as applied to any circumstance, the remainder of this Agreement shall be interpreted so as best to effect the intent of the parties.

7. Integration. This Agreement expresses the complete understanding of the parties with respect to the subject matter and supersedes all prior proposals, agreements, representations and understandings. This Agreement may not be amended except in a writing signed by both parties.

8. Waiver. The failure to exercise any right provided in this Agreement shall not be a waiver of prior or subsequent rights.

This Agreement and each party's obligations shall be binding on the representatives, assigns and successors of each party. Each party has signed this Agreement through its authorized representative.

Disclosing Party:

_____

(Signature)

_____

(Typed or Printed Name)

Date: _____

Evaluating Party:

_____

(Signature)

_____

(Typed or Printed Name)

Title: _____

Date: _____

Option Agreement Provisions

Exclusive Option. Disclosing Party grants to Evaluating Party the exclusive option to enter into an agreement to use the Submission. Evaluating Party shall have_____ months from the date of execution of this Agreement (the "Option Period") to exercise its option for the Submission by signing an agreement incorporating the terms described below.

During the Option Period, Disclosing Party shall not offer or grant any third party any rights to the Submission that will interfere with the exercise of the option granted to Evaluating Party. Evaluating Party shall pay to Disclosing Party the nonrefundable sum of $_____. If Evaluating Party exercises its option, such payment shall be considered as an advance against future payments to Disclosing Party.

[*Alternative 1*]
The agreement to use the Submission shall be substantially similar to that in Attachment A to this Agreement.

[*Alternative 2*]
The agreement to use the Submission shall incorporate the terms set forth below. The parties, acting in good faith, shall use their best efforts to incorporate the terms into a final agreement.

_____

_____

_____

Index

CATALOG

...more from nolo

	PRICE	CODE
BUSINESS		
Avoid Employee Lawsuits (Quick & Legal Series)	$24.95	AVEL
The CA Nonprofit Corporation Kit (Binder w/CD-ROM)	$59.95	CNP
Consultant & Independent Contractor Agreements (Book w/CD-ROM)	$29.95	CICA
The Corporate Minutes Book (Book w/CD-ROM)	$69.95	CORMI
The Employer's Legal Handbook	$39.95	EMPL
Firing Without Fear (Quick & Legal Series)	$29.95	FEAR
Form Your Own Limited Liability Company (Book w/CD-ROM)	$44.95	LIAB
Hiring Independent Contractors: The Employer's Legal Guide (Book w/CD-ROM)	$34.95	HICI
How to Create a Buy-Sell Agreement & Control the Destiny of your Small Business (Book w/Disk-PC)	$49.95	BSAG
How to Form a California Professional Corporation (Book w/CD-ROM)	$59.95	PROF
How to Form a Nonprofit Corporation (Book w/CD-ROM)—National Edition	$44.95	NNP
How to Form a Nonprofit Corporation in California (Book w/CD-ROM)	$44.95	NON
How to Form Your Own California Corporation (Binder w/CD-ROM)	$39.95	CACI
How to Form Your Own California Corporation (Book w/CD-ROM)	$34.95	CCOR
How to Form Your Own New York Corporation (Book w/Disk—PC)	$39.95	NYCO
How to Form Your Own Texas Corporation (Book w/CD-ROM)	$39.95	TCOR
How to Write a Business Plan	$29.95	SBS
The Independent Paralegal's Handbook	$29.95	PARA
Leasing Space for Your Small Business	$34.95	LESP
Legal Guide for Starting & Running a Small Business	$34.95	RUNS
Legal Forms for Starting & Running a Small Business (Book w/CD-ROM)	$29.95	RUNS2
Marketing Without Advertising	$22.00	MWAD
Music Law (Book w/Disk—PC)	$29.95	ML
Nolo's California Quick Corp (Quick & Legal Series)	$19.95	QINC
Nolo's Guide to Social Security Disability	$29.95	QSS
Nolo's Quick LLC (Quick & Legal Series)	$24.95	LLCQ
The Small Business Start-up Kit (Book w/CD-ROM)	$29.95	SMBU
The Small Business Start-up Kit for California (Book w/CD-ROM)	$29.95	OPEN
The Partnership Book: How to Write a Partnership Agreement (Book w/CD-ROM)	$39.95	PART
Sexual Harassment on the Job	$24.95	HARS
Starting & Running a Successful Newsletter or Magazine	$29.95	MAG
Tax Savvy for Small Business	$34.95	SAVVY
Working for Yourself: Law & Taxes for the Self-Employed	$39.95	WAGE
Your Limited Liability Company: An Operating Manual (Book w/Disk—PC)	$49.95	LOP
Your Rights in the Workplace	$29.95	YRW
CONSUMER		
Fed Up with the Legal System: What's Wrong & How to Fix It	$9.95	LEG
How to Win Your Personal Injury Claim	$29.95	PICL
Nolo's Encyclopedia of Everyday Law	$28.95	EVL
Nolo's Pocket Guide to California Law	$15.95	CLAW
Trouble-Free Travel...And What to Do When Things Go Wrong	$14.95	TRAV
ESTATE PLANNING & PROBATE		
8 Ways to Avoid Probate (Quick & Legal Series)	$16.95	PRO8
9 Ways to Avoid Estate Taxes (Quick & Legal Series)	$29.95	ESTX
Estate Planning Basics (Quick & Legal Series)	$18.95	ESPN
How to Probate an Estate in California	$49.95	PAE

	PRICE	CODE
Make Your Own Living Trust (Book w/CD-ROM)	$34.95	LITR
Nolo's Law Form Kit: Wills	$24.95	KWL
Nolo's Simple Will Book (Book w/CD-ROM)	$34.95	SWIL
Plan Your Estate	$39.95	NEST
Quick & Legal Will Book (Quick & Legal Series)	$15.95	QUIC

FAMILY MATTERS

	PRICE	CODE
Child Custody: Building Parenting Agreements That Work	$29.95	CUST
The Complete IEP Guide	$24.95	IEP
Divorce & Money: How to Make the Best Financial Decisions During Divorce	$34.95	DIMO
Do Your Own Divorce in Oregon	$29.95	ODIV
Get a Life: You Don't Need a Million to Retire Well	$24.95	LIFE
The Guardianship Book for California	$34.95	GB
How to Adopt Your Stepchild in California (Book w/CD-ROM)	$34.95	ADOP
A Legal Guide for Lesbian and Gay Couples	$25.95	LG
Living Together: A Legal Guide (Book w/CD-ROM)	$34.95	LTK
Using Divorce Mediation: Save Your Money & Your Sanity	$29.95	UDMD

GOING TO COURT

	PRICE	CODE
Beat Your Ticket: Go To Court and Win! (National Edition)	$19.95	BEYT
The Criminal Law Handbook: Know Your Rights, Survive the System	$29.95	KYR
Everybody's Guide to Small Claims Court (National Edition)	$24.95	NSCC
Everybody's Guide to Small Claims Court in California	$24.95	CSCC
Fight Your Ticket ... and Win! (California Edition)	$24.95	FYT
How to Change Your Name in California	$34.95	NAME
How to Collect When You Win a Lawsuit (California Edition)	$29.95	JUDG
How to Mediate Your Dispute	$18.95	MEDI
How to Seal Your Juvenile & Criminal Records (California Edition)	$34.95	CRIM
Nolo's Deposition Handbook	$29.95	DEP
Represent Yourself in Court: How to Prepare & Try a Winning Case	$34.95	RYC

HOMEOWNERS, LANDLORDS & TENANTS

	PRICE	CODE
California Tenants' Rights	$27.95	CTEN
Contractors' and Homeowners' Guide to Mechanics' Liens (Book w/Disk—PC)—California Edition	$39.95	MIEN
The Deeds Book (California Edition)	$24.95	DEED
Dog Law	$14.95	DOG
Every Landlord's Legal Guide (National Edition, Book w/CD-ROM)	$44.95	ELLI
Every Tenant's Legal Guide	$26.95	EVTEN
For Sale by Owner in California	$29.95	FSBO
How to Buy a House in California	$29.95	BHCA
The Landlord's Law Book, Vol. 1: Rights & Responsibilities (California Edition) (Book w/CD-ROM)	$44.95	LBRT
The California Landlord's Law Book, Vol. 2: Evictions (Book w/CD-ROM)	$44.95	LBEV
Leases & Rental Agreements (Quick & Legal Series)	$24.95	LEAR
Neighbor Law: Fences, Trees, Boundaries & Noise	$24.95	NEI
The New York Landlord's Law Book (Book w/CD-ROM)	$39.95	NYLL
Renters' Rights (National Edition)	$24.95	RENT
Stop Foreclosure Now in California	$29.95	CLOS

HUMOR

	PRICE	CODE
29 Reasons Not to Go to Law School	$12.95	29R
Poetic Justice	$9.95	PJ

IMMIGRATION

	PRICE	CODE
How to Get a Green Card	$29.95	GRN
U.S. Immigration Made Easy	$44.95	IMEZ

MONEY MATTERS

	PRICE	CODE
101 Law Forms for Personal Use (Book w/Disk—PC)	$29.95	SPOT
Bankruptcy: Is It the Right Solution to Your Debt Problems? (Quick & Legal Series)	$19.95	BRS
Chapter 13 Bankruptcy: Repay Your Debts	$34.95	CH13
Creating Your Own Retirement Plan	$29.95	YROP
Credit Repair (Quick & Legal Series, Book w/CD-ROM)	$19.95	CREP
How to File for Chapter 7 Bankruptcy	$34.95	HFB
IRAs, 401(k)s & Other Retirement Plans: Taking Your Money Out	$29.95	RET
Money Troubles: Legal Strategies to Cope With Your Debts	$29.95	MT
Nolo's Law Form Kit: Personal Bankruptcy	$24.95	KBNK
Stand Up to the IRS	$24.95	SIRS
Surviving an IRS Tax Audit (Quick & Legal Series)	$24.95	SAUD
Take Control of Your Student Loan Debt	$24.95	SLOAN

PATENTS AND COPYRIGHTS

	PRICE	CODE
The Copyright Handbook: How to Protect and Use Written Works (Book w/CD-ROM)	$34.95	COHA
Copyright Your Software	$24.95	CYS
Domain Names	$24.95	DOM
Getting Permission: How to License and Clear Copyrighted Materials Online and Off (Book w/Disk—PC)	$34.95	RIPER
How to Make Patent Drawings Yourself	$29.95	DRAW
The Inventor's Notebook	$24.95	INOT
Nolo's Patents for Beginners (Quick & Legal Series)	$29.95	QPAT
License Your Invention (Book w/Disk—PC)	$39.95	LICE
Patent, Copyright & Trademark	$34.95	PCTM
Patent It Yourself	$49.95	PAT
Patent Searching Made Easy	$29.95	PATSE
The Public Domain	$34.95	PUBL
Web and Software Development: A Legal Guide (Book w/ CD-ROM)	$44.95	SFT
Trademark: Legal Care for Your Business and Product Name	$39.95	TRD

RESEARCH & REFERENCE

	PRICE	CODE
Legal Research: How to Find & Understand the Law	$34.95	LRES

SENIORS

	PRICE	CODE
Beat the Nursing Home Trap: A Consumer's Guide to Assisted Living and Long-Term Care	$21.95	ELD
The Conservatorship Book for California	$44.95	CNSV
Social Security, Medicare & Pensions	$24.95	SOA

SOFTWARE
Call or check our website at www.nolo.com for special discounts on Software!

	PRICE	CODE
LeaseWriter CD—Windows	$129.95	LWD1
LLC Maker—Windows	$89.95	LLP1
Personal RecordKeeper 5.0 CD—Windows	$59.95	RKD5
Quicken Lawyer 2002 Business Deluxe—Windows	$79.95	SBQB2
Quicken Lawyer 2002 Personal Deluxe—Windows	$69.95	WQP2

SPECIAL UPGRADE OFFER
Get 35% off the latest edition of your Nolo book

It's important to have the most current legal information. Because laws and legal procedures change often, we update our books regularly. To help keep you up-to-date we are extending this special upgrade offer. Cut out and mail the title portion of the cover of your old Nolo book and we'll give you 35% off the retail price of the NEW EDITION of that book when you purchase directly from us. For more information call us at 1-800-992-6656. This offer is to individuals only.

Order Form

Name _____

Address _____

City _____

State, Zip _____

Daytime Phone _____

E-mail _____

Item Code	Quantity	Item	Unit Price	Total Price

Method of payment

☐ Check   ☐ VISA   ☐ MasterCard
☐ Discover Card   ☐ American Express

Subtotal	
Add your local sales tax (California only)	
Shipping: RUSH $9, Basic $5 (See below)	
"I bought 3, ship it to me FREE!"(Ground shipping only)	
TOTAL	

Account Number _____

Expiration Date _____

Signature _____

Shipping and Handling

Rush Delivery—Only $9

We'll ship any order to any street address in the U.S. by UPS 2nd Day Air* for only $9!

* Order by noon Pacific Time and get your order in 2 business days. Orders placed after noon Pacific Time will arrive in 3 business days. P.O. boxes and S.F. Bay Area use basic shipping. Alaska and Hawaii use 2nd Day Air or Priority Mail.

Basic Shipping—$5

Use for P.O. Boxes, Northern California and Ground Service.

Allow 1-2 weeks for delivery. U.S. addresses only.

For faster service, use your credit card and our toll-free numbers

Order 24 hours a day

Online	www.nolo.com
Phone	1-800-992-6656
Fax	1-800-645-0895
Mail	Nolo
	950 Parker St.
	Berkeley, CA 94710

Visit us online at
www.nolo.com

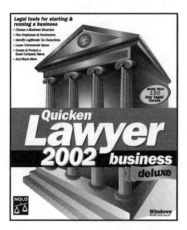

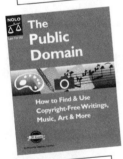
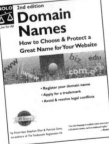

Your comments make a big difference in the development and revision of Nolo books and software. Please take a few minutes and register your Nolo product—and your comments—with us. Not only will your input make a difference, you'll receive special offers available only to registered owners of Nolo products on our newest books and software. Register now by:

PHONE
1-800-992-6656

FAX
1-800-645-0895

EMAIL
cs@nolo.com

or **MAIL** us
this registration card

REMEMBER:
Little publishers have big ears. We really listen to you.

fold here

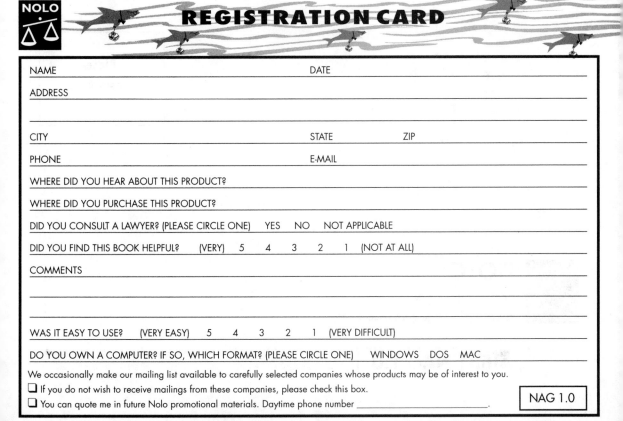

REGISTRATION CARD

NAME	DATE

ADDRESS

CITY	STATE	ZIP

PHONE	E-MAIL

WHERE DID YOU HEAR ABOUT THIS PRODUCT?

WHERE DID YOU PURCHASE THIS PRODUCT?

DID YOU CONSULT A LAWYER? (PLEASE CIRCLE ONE)   YES   NO   NOT APPLICABLE

DID YOU FIND THIS BOOK HELPFUL?   (VERY)   5   4   3   2   1   (NOT AT ALL)

COMMENTS

WAS IT EASY TO USE?   (VERY EASY)   5   4   3   2   1   (VERY DIFFICULT)

DO YOU OWN A COMPUTER? IF SO, WHICH FORMAT? (PLEASE CIRCLE ONE)   WINDOWS   DOS   MAC

We occasionally make our mailing list available to carefully selected companies whose products may be of interest to you.
❑ If you do not wish to receive mailings from these companies, please check this box.
❑ You can quote me in future Nolo promotional materials. Daytime phone number _____.

NAG 1.0

NOLO IN THE *NEWS*

"Nolo helps lay people perform legal tasks without the aid—or fees—of lawyers."

—USA TODAY

Nolo books are ..."written in plain language, free of legal mumbo jumbo, and spiced with witty personal observations."

—ASSOCIATED PRESS

"...Nolo publications...guide people simply through the how, when, where and why of law."

—WASHINGTON POST

"Increasingly, people who are not lawyers are performing tasks usually regarded as legal work... And consumers, using books like Nolo's, do routine legal work themselves."

—NEW YORK TIMES

"...All of [Nolo's] books are easy-to-understand, are updated regularly, provide pull-out forms...and are often quite moving in their sense of compassion for the struggles of the lay reader."

—SAN FRANCISCO CHRONICLE

fold here

- -

 nolo

950 Parker Street
Berkeley, CA 94710-9867

Attn: | NAG 1.0 |